THE QUEST FOR HAPPINESS

FINDING THE MEANING OF LIFE
WITHIN GOD'S PLAN

Sam + Nancy,
May God bless you,
The O'Hearns

THE QUEST FOR HAPPINESS

FINDING THE MEANING OF LIFE WITHIN GOD'S PLAN

Venerable Louis of Granada

Edited and arranged by
Ryan Grant

TAN Books
Gastonia, NC

Cover & interior design by www.davidferrisdesign.com

Cover Image: *Portrait of Fray Luis de Granada in Francisco Pacheco*, 1564-1644, Royal Academy of History (Madrid), Public domain, Wikimedia Commons

ISBN: 978-150511-716-5

Published in the United States by

TAN Books
PO Box 410487
Charlotte, NC 28241

www.TANBooks.com

Printed in the United States of America

TABLE OF CONTENTS

Editor's Note VII

The Meaning of Life..1

False Happiness of This World 7

True Happiness.. 15

Living a Life of Virtue 21

The Gifts of the Holy Spirit...................................... 28

Venial and Mortal Sin 34

Sins Against the Holy Spirit 48

The Slavery of Sin 55

Manual for Avoiding Sin 61

God's Law.. 70

Divine Grace 75

Justification Through Grace...................................... 87

EDITOR'S NOTE

W HAT is the meaning of life? What is love? How can I be happy? These are questions that people today often ask rhetorically, as though there were no answers. Others hunt down answers in self-help books, guides from experts, or television. Films and novels explore these themes but give no satisfying answer, rather they merely conclude with a nice emotional ending. But reality isn't so. There is a bit of reality that is lacking in a secular culture that relies upon man alone, and this engenders the questions above. What is lacking is God, and an understanding of reality where the world is concerned. To make relationships work, above all our relationship with God, we must break the cycle of sin and unbelief.

The great Dominican, Venerable Louis of Granada, also understood this. Best known for his work *The Sinner's Guide*, Granada wrote this treatise, *The Quest for Happiness*, as part of his *Summa of the Christian Life*, following a consideration of virtue and God's creation.

Though his 16th century Spain was quite Catholic on the surface, it was still plagued with worldly thinking and a trust on man's own work to bring about happiness—a very temporary happiness at that—which is overshadowed by the evils of the world. Sin, violence, the destructive behavior of our neighbors, and our destructive behavior towards them, all flow from failing to grasp the reality of our final end, which is God Himself.

Thus, he lays out his work, *The Quest for Happiness* with this view in mind. What is the meaning of life? It is not a rhetorical question, rather, the Church has the answer! To know, love and serve almighty God. But when this doesn't happen, and we turn to the world, what unhappiness follows, as de Granada shows, due to the fact that this world cannot give happiness, and we are then in the grip of sin and its effects. What course do we follow? This book gives the answer of how to proceed on such a quest out of the unhappiness of the world and toward the happiness of God.

With this in mind, we have prepared this new edition of the Venerable Louis of Granada's work, lightly edited and adjusted for the problems that modern man faces today. May it help many souls navigate the wasteland of modernity toward true happiness, which is God.

—*The Editor*

CHAPTER 1

THE MEANING OF LIFE

THERE are many who develop a "way of life," or a new philosophy that proposes to make one a good person without religion. Others like to say they are spiritual but not religious, and this is enough to be good and moral. While these have a pleasant ring to the ear, these ideas are insufficient for enabling men to live well, because they lack a proper notion of man's final end. To understand man's true goal, we must know that all men are born with a desire to reach a state where they will be so completely satisfied that would desire nothing else. Such a state is called happiness or beatitude. Ancient philosophers did not doubt that it was possible to arrive at such a state, seeing that even they understood the Author of nature would not impress on our hearts a natural desire for something that is impossible to obtain. Modern, who takes it for granted that he can get there by being good in an anomalous sense, still man hopes for it, they even long for it. God did not place such desires in us for no reason.

Both ancients and moderns, knowing there is something else after death, do everything they can to discover what can provide this perfect happiness. They know that they cannot order their lives well unless they knew the meaning of human life. In things that are directed to certain purpose, we must determine what to do from this very purpose. In this way, a pilot must know to what place he is flying the plane so that it actually gets there. So also, to properly direct human life a man must first know his ultimate end so that he may direct all his steps toward it. Among the ancient philosophers, Aristotle first treated on man's ultimate end to discover the rules for a good life, because the final goal of human life determines the plan and rules that must be proposed for getting there.

Furthermore, many of the ancient philosophers made every effort to discover how man's ultimate end would be found. Nevertheless, they all differed with one another, and they could count hundreds of ideas about the meaning of life. Some observed that man is neither a pure spirit nor a mere body, rather a body-soul composite, so they concluded that man's happiness is to be found in a blending of the goods of body and soul. Since the soul possesses two principal faculties—the intellect and the will—they required perfect wisdom in the intellect and complete virtue in the will. In the body he would require health, power, proper disposition of its parts, and a good temperament.

Lastly, this conception of some of the ancients presupposes freedom from all the evils and miseries of this life, seeing that such things would disturb the soul and be detrimental to the goods of the body that are required for perfect happiness.

St. Augustine refers to these opinions in his City of God, but he scoffs at the folly of placing man's true happiness in a life that is surrounded by misery and misfortune. If happiness consists in certain goods of body and soul and in freedom from all evils, how will we ever find a man who is perfectly happy? This life is a sea of constant change, a vale of tears, wherein there are more miseries than there are hairs on a man's head. Man is plagued by afflictions of the body and unruly desires in the soul. He experiences anger and hatred because of injuries received and disappointment in not getting the goods which he wants. His life is made sorrowful by the death of loved ones, the injuries endured at the hands of wicked neighbors, the betrayals and deceptions of false friends, and injustices from civil authorities. How can he find perfect happiness in a life where there is so little truth, so little faith, so little loyalty?

Then, what shall we say of the constant war of the flesh against the spirit, the temptations of the devil, the cruel wars on land, sea and air that destroy the peace of men and nations, not to mention the intrigues and false testimony of perverse men, the tyranny of the powerful, and the oppression of the weak? Observing the sufferings of this life, Solomon considered the dead to be in a happier state than the living,[1] and Job, a man who knew suffering well, states that "the life of man upon earth is a warfare and his days are like the days of a hireling."[2]

If perfect wisdom is needed for perfect happiness, how many years and how much study will be necessary to obtain it! A man would be fortunate indeed if he succeeded in acquiring true wisdom by the time he reached old age. If, in addition to wisdom, perfect virtue is required—and for this it is necessary to mortify the passions and have them under perfect control—who could reach such a state without divine grace? If, besides these perfections of intellect and will, perfect happiness demanded certain perfections of the body, when and where shall we find all these perfections together? Sometimes, one deficiency can make a man more miserable than all the other perfections can make him happy, as is clearly demonstrated in Scripture, where we read that Aman, in spite of all his wealth, his multitude of children, and the great honor that had been paid to him by Esther, felt that he had nothing, as long as Mordechai refused to show him honor and reverence.[3] If it is so difficult to find all these perfections in one man, who will be truly happy? Yet, if all animals can obtain their proper ends, it would be a cruel irony if man alone, for whom this visible universe was created, were unable to reach his ultimate goal.

---

1 - Eccles. 4:2.

2 - Job 7:1.

3 - Esther 5:9-13.

What shall we say of modern thinkers? Rather than seeking pure perfections, they seek a perfection of feelings, satisfied in adding random meditations, combined with new philosophies or methods of life that sound good, but do not ultimately satisfy the soul.

Both have erred, and they deserve both pardon and blame. They can be excused to the extent that they knew nothing about the happiness of the next life and were forced to seek for it in this life. Some place happiness in one line of goods and others in another, depending upon their personal inclinations and tastes. But pressed as they were to find a solution, they are deserving of blame for not seeking light from the Creator so that they could arrive at the truth. Relying on their own ingenuity, they not only believed that they could understand what makes true happiness, but that they could attain this happiness by their own efforts.

We can draw two conclusions from all this. The first is that man is able to attain the state of perfect happiness, but since this happiness is not to be found in this life, it must be found in the life to come; otherwise man's natural desire for beatitude would be fruitless and in vain. The knowledge of this truth is so important that the St. Paul makes it the very foundation of Christianity: "A man that comes to God must believe that He exists, and rewards those who seek Him."[4]

---

4 - Hebrews 11:6.

The second conclusion has to do with the fact of divine revelation. Philosophies, fashions, feelings, or being "spiritual" are not sufficient to teach either the true religion or to give us the rules for a good life. If philosophers, both ancient and modern, have been unable to discover the true meaning of life, they cannot teach us how to discover it, since the means are determined by the end. On the other hand, if divine providence is not lacking in the care of the animals, how could it be lacking to the most noble of all God's visible creatures in regard to that one, most necessary thing? It is of the utmost importance for man to know how he should honor and serve God, and that he should know the purpose for which he was created, as well as the means of attaining that end. Therefore, it is not fitting that the Creator should fail man in this great need of his soul, while providing for the needs of the body, since it would be contrary to His wisdom and providence if He were to care for those things that are more lowly while at the same time, to neglect what is more noble. Such a disorder is incompatible with God's infinite goodness and wisdom. We conclude from this that it pertains to the perfection of divine providence to reveal to us this truth concerning His glory and our beatitude, and to teach us the way to happiness and salvation.

CHAPTER 2

FALSE HAPPINESS OF THIS WORLD

IF we stop and consider the happiness of this world, we will find that it is mixed with many kinds of evil. Firstly, no matter how good it may be, Man's earthly happiness is very brief. It cannot last any longer than his life, and however long his life may be, it rarely reaches a hundred years. St. John Chrysostom tells us, "Let us devote a hundred years to the pleasures of this world, then another hundred, and then twice again another hundred; how does all this compare with eternity?"

Even evil men have admitted this: "So we also being born, forthwith ceased to be, ... but are consumed in our wickedness."[5] Look at how short the wicked will find that their whole lives appear to be when they enter eternity. It

---

5 - Wisd. 5:13.

will seem to them that they have hardly lived a day, as if they had been carried from the womb to the tomb. The pleasures of this world will then seem to them merely a dream of joys that never really were. "And as he that is hungry dreams and eats, but when he is awake his soul is empty, and as he that is thirsty dreams and drinks, but after he is awake his soul is yet faint with thirst and his soul is empty, so shall be the multitude of all the Gentiles that have fought against Mount Sion."[6]

"Where," says Baruch, "are the princes of the nations and they that rule over the beasts that are on the earth, that take their diversion with the birds of the air, that hoard silver and gold wherein men trust and there is no end of their getting, who work in silver and are solicitous and their works are unsearchable? They are cut off and are gone down to hell, and others are risen up in their place."[7] Where is the wise and educated man? What has become of the glory of Solomon? Where is the powerful Alexander the Great? Where are the Caesars? Where are the great kings and statesmen of the world? What did all of their, worldly power, great wealth, legions of soldiers, and companies of flatterers get them? All this was but dust, a happiness that passed in a moment.

Another evil that mingles itself with this world's happiness is the many miseries in this vale of tears. Truly, the miseries of man are more numerous than the days or hours

---

6 - Isa. 29:8.

7 - Bar. 3:16-19.

of his life. Each day brings its cares and each hour threatens us with its misery. Who could count all the diseases that afflict us? Or the annoyances caused by our neighbors? You get in an argument with one person, another attacks you, and a third ruins your good name. Some hate you, others treat you with envy and deceit, and others with desire for revenge. All of them make war against you until the end.

In addition to these miseries there is an infinite number of unexpected disasters and misfortunes. One man loses his sight, another breaks an arm, another falls from a high place, another drowns, and yet another loses a fortune. If you want more, ask the men of the world how their brief pleasures have brought many griefs in their wake. For if the two were to be weighed together, you would see that the one far outweighs the other and that for one hour of pleasure there are a hundred hours of grief.

But these miseries are common to both the good and the bad, for all men cross the same ocean of life, and are subject to the same storms. There are other miseries that afflict only evil men, for they are the daughters of the evil deeds these men commit. If we look to these miseries, it is clear how horrible the life of sin really is. Sinners themselves admit the magnitude of their misery, as we read in the Book of Wisdom: "We wearied ourselves in the way of iniquity and destruction, and have walked through hard ways, but the way of the Lord we did not know. What has pride profited us? Or what advantage has the boasting of riches brought us? All those things are passed away like a shadow ... and as a ship that passes through the waves, and when it is gone by, the trace cannot be found nor the path of its keel in the waters; or as when a bird flies through the air, of the passage of which no mark can be found, but only the sound of the wings beating the light air, and parting it by the force of her flight. ... So we also being born, right away cease to be and have been able to show no mark of virtue, but are consumed in our wickedness."[8] Consequently, as the good in this life enjoy a kind of paradise and yet look forward to another, so the sinners have a hell in this life and await another in the life to come.

If it were merely a question of the pains and labors of this life, that would not be cause for excessive fear. Yet, there are also dangers to the soul, and these are much harder to bear because they touch us more vitally. Thus, we read in Scripture: "He shall rain snares upon sinners."[9] Since sinners have so little guard over their hearts and senses, and are so careless in avoiding the occasions of sin, how can they avoid walking into countless dangers? This is why God rains snares upon the wicked; snares in their youth and snares in their old age; snares in riches and in poverty; snares in honor and snares in dishonor; snares in their association with other men and snares in solitude; snares in adversity and snares in prosperity.

---

8 - Wisd. 5:7-13.

9 - Ps. 10:7.

Who, then, will not fear such a dangerous world? Who will not be afraid to walk unarmed among so many enemies and unprotected amid so many occasions of sin? Who will consider himself secure?

To this multitude of snares and dangers we may add yet another misery which makes them even greater: the blindness and darkness of worldly persons, which is fittingly symbolized by the darkness recorded in the land of Egypt during the time of Moses.[10] So dense was this darkness that for three days no man could see his neighbor nor move out of the place where he was. This is the same darkness which the world suffers, only it is much worse. What greater blindness than for so many men to believe as they do and yet to live as they do? What greater blindness than to think so much of men and take so little notice of God? Knowing for certain that we must die and that the moment of death will determine our state for all eternity, what greater blindness could there be than to live as carelessly as if we were to live forever? What greater blindness than to forego the heritage of heaven for the satisfaction of our feelings? Men have eyes sharper than an eagle's for the things of this world but are blinder than moles in regard to the things of heaven.

Since there are so many snares in the world, what can be expected but many sins and falls? Cast your eyes on the palaces, cities, and nations of the world; you will see so many sins, such forgetfulness of God, and such disregard

---

10 - Exod. 10:21.

for one's own salvation that you will be astonished at so much evil. You will see that the greater part of men live like animals, following the impulse of their passions, without any more regard for the laws of justice than those who have no knowledge of God and think that there is nothing for man but birth and death. You will see the innocent mistreated, the guilty excused, the good despised, sinners honored and praised, the poor and humble oppressed, and human respect esteemed above virtue. You will see that laws are flouted, truth is ignored, shame is lost, the arts are corrupted, political office is abused, and the states of life are perverted. You will see how evil men, by means of corruption, theft, deceit, and other unlawful deeds, acquire great wealth and are feared and praised by all, while others, who scarcely deserve to be called men, are chosen for high office. You will see that men love and worship their money more than they do God and for its sake they violate every human and divine law, so that nothing remains of justice but its name.

When you have witnessed all these things, you will understand with what good reason the Psalmist could say: "The Lord looked down from heaven upon the children of men, to see if there be any that understand and seek God. They are all gone aside; they are become unprofitable together. There is none that does good; no not one."[11] Likewise did Hosea complain: "There is no truth and there is no mercy and there is no knowledge of God in the land.

---

11 - Ps. 13:2-3.

Cursing and lying and killing and theft and adultery have overflowed, and blood hath touched blood."[12]

Who would not wish to abandon such a world? Certainly Jeremiah had such a desire when he said: "Who will give me a lodging for travelers in the wilderness, and I will leave my people and depart from them? Because they are all adulterers, an assembly of transgressors, and they have bent their tongue as a bow, for lies and not for truth; they have strengthened themselves upon the earth, for they have proceeded from evil to evil, and Me they have not known, says the Lord."[13]

These and many others are the miseries and evils that accompany the wretched happiness of this world, and through them you can perceive how much more bitterness than sweetness it carries with it. Besides being brief and wretched, the happiness of this world is also filthy, because it makes men carnal and impure; it is brutish, because it makes men beasts; it is foolish, because it makes men fools and often deprives them of reason; and it is faithless and treacherous, because when we are enjoying it most, it leaves us and vanishes into the air.

Lastly, this world's happiness is false and deceptive. It appears to be what it is not and it promises to give what it cannot. In this way, it lures many souls to eternal ruin. Just as there are true gold and false gold, true jewels and glass, so there are true goods and apparent goods, true happiness

---

12 - Hos. 4:1-2.

13 - Jer. 9:2-3.

and that which appears to be happiness but is not. Such is the happiness of this world, and for that reason ignorant persons are easily deceived, as fish are caught with the bait. It is the nature of physical things to present themselves to us under a pleasant guise and with an attractive appearance which promise joy and contentment, but when experience undeceives us, we feel the hook beneath the bait.

Accordingly, what is all the happiness of the world but a siren's song which lulls one to sleep? If it delights, it is to deceive us; if it lifts us up, it is to cast us down again; if it gladdens us, it is to sadden us. It gives pleasure at an exorbitant rate of interest. Its tranquility is distressing, its security is without foundation, its fear is without cause, its labors without fruit, its tears without purpose, its projects without success, its hope vain, its joy fictitious, and its sorrow true.

In all this you can see how much this world is like hell itself, for if hell is a place of pain and torment, what else abounds more in this world? This is the fruit of the world; this is the merchandise that it sells; this is the treatment that one receives on every side. So St. Bernard said that were it not for the hope we have of obtaining a better life, this world would seem little better than hell itself.

CHAPTER 3

TRUE HAPPINESS

NOW that we have seen how wretched the happiness of this world is, it remains for us to consider that true happiness can be found only in God. If worldly men understood this well, they would not pursue earthly pleasures as they do.

No creature can enjoy perfect happiness until it attains its ultimate end, that is, the last perfection that is due to it according to its nature. Until it arrives at this state, it is necessarily restless and discontented, just as anyone who feels a need for that which he yet lacks. Now, what is the ultimate end of man, the possession of which constitutes his complete happiness, the very meaning of life? Undoubtedly, it is God, who is man's first beginning and last end. And just as it is impossible for man to have two beginnings, it is likewise impossible to have two ultimate ends, because that would mean there must be two gods.

So, if God alone is man's last end and true happiness, it is impossible for man to find true happiness outside of God. As the glove is made for the hand, and it serves no other purpose than the one for which it was made, so the human heart, created as it is for God, cannot find rest in anything outside of God. It is content in Him alone, and without Him it is poor and needy. The reason for this is man's perfect happiness especially consists in the operation of his most noble faculties, intellect and will, and as long as these are restless, man himself cannot be calm and content. But these two faculties can never be at rest except in God alone. St. Thomas says that our intellect cannot know and understand so much as not to be capable and desirous of knowing more, if there is more to be known, and our will cannot love and enjoy so many goods as not to be capable of more, if more can be given. Consequently, these two faculties will never be satisfied until they find a universal object in which there are to be found everything that, once it is known and loved, will leave no more truths to be known and no more goods to be loved. It follows from this that no created thing, not even the possession of the entire universe, can satisfy our heart, but only Him for whom it was created—God.

To bring out this truth more clearly, think of a needle on a compass. The needle has been touched with a magnet and as a result it always points to the north. Observe how restless this needle is and how it fluctuates until it points to the north. Once this is done, the needle stops and remains fixed. So also, God created man with a natural compass, with God as the true North, and as long as man is separated from God, he remains restless, even though he possess all the treasures of the world. But once he has turned to God, he finds repose, just as the needle when it turns north, for in God man finds all his rest. Hence, he alone is happy who possesses God. Since in this life the just are closer to God, they are the more happy, even if the world does not understand their happiness.

The next argument is based on the principle that much more is required to make a thing perfect than to make it imperfect, for perfection requires that a thing be completely perfect, but imperfection requires only one defect. Moreover, perfect happiness requires a man to have all that he desires, and if only one thing is missing, this may contribute more to his unhappiness than do all the other things to his happiness. Sometimes people in high places with great possessions who, in spite of these things, were most unhappy because they were made more wretched by what they wanted and could not obtain than they were made happy by all that they had. However much a man may have, it will not give him satisfaction as long as he is tormented by a desire for something. It is not the possession of many things that makes a man happy, but the satisfaction and fulfillment of all his desires.

St. Augustine explained this beautifully when he wrote: "To my way of thinking, no man can be called truly happy who has not obtained what he loves, whatever it may be. He cannot be happy when he does not love what he possesses, even if the thing he possesses is very good. A man who desires something he cannot obtain remains wretched and tormented. A man who desires what is not worth desiring, deceives himself. A man who does not desire what should be desired is sick. From this it follows that our happiness consists in the possession and love of the supreme good and apart from this no man can be happy." Therefore, these three things, possession and love and the supreme good, make a man happy. Apart from this no man can be happy no matter how much he possesses.

If this be true, the Psalmist is right to sing: "O sons of men, how long will you be dull of heart? Why do you love vanity and seek after lying?"[14] He says both vanity and to lying, because if the things of this world were merely vanity, which is to be nothing, this would be a minor evil, but what is worse, they are also lies and deception, for they make us believe they are something when in reality they are nothing. Hence, Solomon says: "Favor is deceitful and beauty is vain."[15]

All this is proof of the hypocrisy of the world. Hypocrites strive to cover up their faults, and in this way, worldly men try to hide the true misery that they suffer. The first try to pass themselves off as saints, when in reality they are sinners; the second try to appear happy, when

---

14 –   Ps. 4:3.

15 –   Prov. 31:30.

18

in reality they are wretched. If you look upon the grandeur of their state and the splendor of their homes, you will think they are the happiest of men, but if you come a little closer, you will find that they are very different from what they appear to be. As a result, many who wanted to obtain a high station in life, or great possessions, later reject all such things when they have had the opportunity to discover the thorns that lie hidden beneath the flower. Then we find those who live contrary to God's commands in Scripture, who declare they are happy. They may be content with their possessions and their associations with others, but they all know there is something missing. They cannot or will not put their finger on what it is, but it is the absence of their divine creator, however much they content themselves otherwise.

O sons of men, created in the image of God, redeemed by His blood, and destined to become companions of the angels, why do you love vanity and seek after lies, thinking that you can find rest in those false goods that never have given happiness and never will? Why have you left the banquet of the angels for the food of beasts? Why have you left the delights and perfumes of paradise for the bitterness and stench of this world? Have not the calamities and disasters of daily life made you want to escape from the cruel tyranny of this world?

We sometimes act like certain unfortunate women that have fallen in love with a man who is worthless, who dines and frolics with them at his good pleasure and beats and mistreats them every day, and yet in spite of such wretched subjection and slavery, they still pursue him. If we cannot find true happiness in this world but only in God, why don't we seek it in Him? "Cross the earth and the sea, or travel where you will," says St. Augustine, "wherever you go, you will be miserable if you do not go to God."

CHAPTER 4

LIVING A LIFE OF VIRTUE

TO understand how the virtues work in our life, we should recall that virtuous acts can be reduced to two types. The first are spiritual and internal, the second are visible and external. In the first kind we place the acts of the theological virtues, which have God as their object and of which charity has the first place as queen of all the others. To these we may add acts of humility, chastity, mercy, patience, discretion, devotion, poverty of spirit, contempt of the world, denial of self-will and love of the Cross, and similar virtuous acts. We call them spiritual and internal because they are immanent operations, although they may also be manifested externally.

The second type of virtues comprises acts that are visible and external, such as fasting, discipline, silence, solitude, spiritual reading, prayer, chanting, pilgrimages, hearing Mass, listening to sermons, and all the observances and bodily ceremonies of the Christian and religious life. Although these acts also are primarily in the soul, their proper acts are more external than those of the first type of virtues, whose acts are often hidden and invisible, such as to believe, to love, to hope, to contemplate, to humble oneself interiorly, to have sorrow for sins, to judge prudently, and so forth.

Of these two classes of virtuous acts there is no doubt that the first is more excellent and more necessary than the second. As Christ said to the Samaritan women: "The hour comes, and now is, when the true adorers shall adore the Father in spirit and in truth. For the Father also seeks such to adore Him. God is a spirit, and they that adore Him must adore Him in spirit and in truth."[16]

Although most of the attention is given to the internal acts of virtue, the external acts, although of lesser excellence, are very important. Solitude and prevents a man from seeing, hearing, and discussing a thousand things that would be dangerous not only for his peace and tranquility, but also for his chastity and innocence. Silence is a great aid to devotion and prevents many sins of speech, as we read in Scripture: "In the multitude of words there shall no lack of sin; but he that seals his lips is most wise."[17] Fasting, besides being an act of the virtue of temperance and a meritorious work, if done under the impulse of charity, subdues the body, lifts the spirit, lessens the power

---

16 – John 4:23–24.

17 – Prov. 10:19.

LIVING A LIFE OF VIRTUE

of the adversary, disposes us for prayer, spiritual reading, and contemplation, saves us from the excesses of those who are overly fond of eating and drinking and from the reproaches, loquacity, and quarrels that arise after men are satiated. The reading of holy books, attendance at sermons, participation in prayer, singing hymns, and assistance at Divine Office are acts of religion and incentives to devotion and they serve to enlighten the intellect and inflame the will for spiritual things.

If you adhere to the doctrine we have expounded, you will avoid two extremes: that of the Pharisees and that of the Luther's followers. The Pharisees, a carnal and ambitious group who could see nothing but the external observance of the law, took no account of true justice, which is a spiritual and internal virtue. This is why they had only the appearance of virtue without its substance, appearing good on the outside while within they were abominable. The followers of Luther, on the other hand, having seen the error of the Pharisees, fled from one extreme to the other and rejected and disdained all external acts of virtue. But Catholic doctrine avoids these two extremes by giving proper recognition to both the internal and the external virtues, but it gives the internal virtues first place while not neglecting to give the external virtues the importance that is due them.

What is more deserving of love than virtue, where all perfections are to be found? What is more deserving of honor than virtue? If the beauty of virtue could be seen, it would draw the whole world after it. What is more useful and a greater basis for hope than virtue, whereby we obtain our highest good? What greater delight is there than a good conscience? What greater delight than the consolations of the Holy Spirit which accompany virtue? The just man will be remembered for all eternity but the name of the wicked will corrupt and disappear like smoke. There is no greater wisdom than to know God and to know how to travel through life, using the right means to attain one's ultimate end. Thus, the virtuous life causes a beauty that is pleasing not only to God and the angels but even to the wicked and one's own enemies

The good of virtue is so absolute that it has nothing of evil in it. "Say to the just man that it is well."[18] Tell him that he was born in a propitious hour and that he will die in a propitious hour. Tell him that he shall be blessed in his life as well as in his death and in that which will follow after death. Tell him that he shall prosper in all things, in his pleasures and pains, in his labor and rest, and in his honors and dishonors, because for those who love God all things work together unto good. Tell him that although all the world be evil, he has nothing to fear, because the day of his redemption is at hand. Tell him that it is well, because the greatest of all goods, God Himself, is prepared for him and he is freed from the devil, who is the greatest of evils and man's worst enemy.

---

18 - Isa. 3:10.

The just man's name is written in the book of life. God the Father takes him as His son, God the Son takes him as His brother, and the Holy Spirit takes him as His living temple. Truly, the path that he has taken and the resolution he has followed have worked out to his good: good for his soul and good for his body; good in the estimation of God and of men; good for this life and good for the life to come, because to those who seek first the kingdom of God, all things else shall be added. And even if some temporal affairs do not go well with the just man, they also will be to his greater good if they are borne with patience, because to those who have patience, losses become gains, sufferings bring merit, and battles win crowns.

Why would you be so cruel to yourself and so much your own enemy that you do not embrace something that is in every way to your own advantage? What better counsel could you take than the following? "Blessed are the undefiled in the way, who walk in the law of the Lord. Blessed are they that search His testimonies; that seek Him with their whole heart."[19] If, as the philosophers say, good is the object of our will and if better things are more deserving of our love, who has so vitiated your will that you do not embrace the great good of virtue? If you consider your obligation, is there any greater than that which you owe to God simply because He is what He is? If you look for benefits, what greater benefits than those we have received from God, for not only did He create us and

---

19 - Ps. 118:1-2.

redeem us with His own blood, but everything we have, body, soul, life, health, grace, good desires and resolutions, everything proceeds from Him who is the source of goodness. If you are motivated by self-interest, let all the angels and men declare whether there is anything more beneficial to us than eternal glory and freedom from everlasting torment, which is the reward of virtue.

We shall conclude this matter by quoting from a beautiful letter written by St. Cyprian: "There is but one peaceful and secure tranquility and but one firm and perpetual security: when a man, freed from the storms and tempests of this world and placed in the secure haven and port of salvation, lifts his eyes from earth to heaven and, already admitted to the grace and companionship of the Lord, delights to see how all that which was esteemed in the opinion of the world has fallen to ruins in his heart. Such a man cannot desire anything of the world because he is now above the world. ... It is not necessary to have many riches or ambitious projects to obtain this happiness; it is a gift of God which is bestowed on the devout soul.... Whence you, my brother, who are already enlisted in this heavenly army, work with all your energy to observe faithfully the discipline of this army by means of the Christian exercises. Take as your constant companions spiritual reading and prayer; sometimes speaking to God and at other times letting God speak to you. Let Him teach you His commandments; let Him dispose and order all the affairs of your life. Whomever God enriches, let no one consider poor.... All the edifices made of precious marble or laid over with gold will appear to you as dung when you understand that it is you who should first be adorned and that this is a much more magnificent structure wherein God reposes as in a living temple and which the Holy Spirit has taken as His dwelling place. Let us, then, decorate this house with innocence; let us brighten it with the light and splendor of justice…. It will not deteriorate or tarnish, but will become even more beautiful with the resurrection of the body."

CHAPTER 5

THE GIFTS OF THE HOLY SPIRIT

THE HOLY SPIRIT governs the just and strengthens and sustains them in their spiritual life through His gifts. The gifts of the Holy Spirit are seven in number: wisdom, understanding, counsel, fortitude, knowledge, piety, and fear of the Lord. In showing how these seven gifts were perfectly blended in Christ and in His mystical body, the Church, Isaias says: "There shall come forth a rod out of the root of Jesse, and a flower shall rise up out of His root. And the Spirit of the Lord shall rest upon Him: the spirit of wisdom and of understanding, the spirit of counsel and of fortitude, the spirit of knowledge and of godliness, and He shall be filled with the spirit of the fear of the Lord."[20]

---

20 - Isa. 11:1-2.

The gifts proceed in an orderly fashion and gradually ascend by degrees. From the fear of the Lord, the soul rises to the other gifts, one after the other, to arrive at the loftiest and best of all, which is the gift of wisdom. We must speak of "fear of the Lord", because the name suggests a worldly and servile fear. Really, it is an awe that awakens in us a knowledge of Who God is, not a cowering fear which the Apostle calls the spirit of bondage.[21] Fear of the Lord, properly understood, means to be among the adopted sons of God. This fear enables the Christian to venerate his merciful Father with filial reverence, striving conscientiously never to offend Him in the slightest way nor to lose His grace and love. St. Augustine calls it a chaste fear which is born of charity.

The gift of piety teaches and inclines us to honor God with ardent and joyful affection and to love our neighbor for the love of God, even when he is not deserving of our love. The gift of knowledge impels us to recognize our defects and learn how to live innocently and prudently in this evil world without committing sin. The gift of fortitude enables us to remain strong and constant in Christ, so that neither the pleasures nor the difficulties of this world can separate us in any way from the honor and service of God. It makes us yearn and thirst for the just life.

The gift of counsel teaches, advises, and directs us to diligently put into effect what we prudently judge to be

---

21 - Rom. 8:15.

most conducive to our salvation and for the greater glory of God. The gift of understanding discloses to us the true and Catholic meaning of divine matters. Through the gift of wisdom, the soul is completely detached from all earthly things so that it may enjoy the contemplation of God and experience the most tender consolation, as well as a longing for divine delights.

We should beg God to stir up these gifts in our souls through the merits of Jesus Christ, His Son, from whom they flow as from an abundant spring. So the Savior tells us: "If you, then, being evil, know how to give good gifts to your children, how much more will your Father from heaven give the good Spirit to them that ask Him?"[22] And St. James says: "If any of you want wisdom, let him ask of God, who gives to all men abundantly and does not upbraid, and it shall be given him. But let him ask in faith, nothing wavering."[23]

The gifts of the Holy Spirit also guides the work of the virtues, animating and strengthening them so that they will always be ready for the performance of their proper acts. Faith, hope, and charity are perfected by the gifts of wisdom and understanding; prudence, by the gifts of knowledge and counsel; justice, by the gift of piety; fortitude, by the gift of fortitude; and temperance, by the fear of the Lord.

---

22 – Luke 11:13.

23 – Jas 1:5-6.

The gifts also help to destroy the seven evil inclinations which the prince of devils arouses in those who live according to the desires of the flesh and the law of sin. Thus, the fear of the Lord destroys pride and prepares a man for true humility, as Solomon says: "The fruit of humility is fear of the Lord."[24] The gift of piety, which makes us desire the good of our neighbor with a joyful heart, replaces envy, as St. Peter says: "In patience, godliness; and in godliness, love of brotherhood."[25] The gift of knowledge represses anger, which is usually accompanied by folly, as it is written: "Be not quick to anger, for anger rests in the bosom of a fool."[26] A man that has the gift of knowledge understands that he must not be angry at those who have unjustly offended him, but that he must treat them as one treats children, the sick, or those who are mentally challenged. Thus, parents, friends, and doctors are the objects of much abuse and recrimination, but they suffer it all with patience, and will even endure much more until the sick have regained their health or those who suffer mentally have been restored to sanity.

The gift of fortitude dissipates the spirit of sloth as well as spiritual sadness and rids the soul of its morbid boredom. It brightens and gladdens the soul and sustains it in hope, as Isaias says: "In silence and in hope shall your

---

24 - Prov. 22:4.

25 - Cf. 2 Pet. 1:5-8.

26 - Eccles. 7:10.

strength be."[27] Likewise we read in the Book of Ezra: "Be not sad; for the joy of the Lord is our strength."[28] And St. James writes: "Are any of you sad? Let him pray. Let him sing."[29]

The spirit of counsel uproots avarice, because anyone that is instructed by this gift will willingly choose what is better. He enriches his soul with spiritual goods and lays up treasures in heaven where they can never be lost, instead of gathering the riches of the earth, which the worms eat, the moths consume, or thieves steal. To this effect, the Savior asked: "What shall it profit a man, if he gain the whole world, and suffer the loss of his soul?"[30] The gift of understanding destroys gluttony, which enslaves those who give themselves to this vice, as we read in Scripture: "Do not become like the horse and the mule, who have no understanding."[31] The gift of wisdom destroys lust, for they who possess the spirit of wisdom delight in God and abhor the pleasures of carnal men, who are like beasts in their own excrement.[32]

Let us, therefore, beg God, our Father, to grant us these seven gifts through the merits of His Son, Jesus Christ, saying with the Psalmist: "Create a clean heart in me, O God,

---

27 – Isa. 30:15.

28 – 2 Ez. 8:10.

29 – Jas. 5:13.

30 – Mark 8:36.

31 – Ps. 31:9.

32 – Cf. Joel 1:17.

and renew a right spirit within my bowels. Cast me not away from Thy face and take not Thy Holy Spirit from me. Restore unto me the joy of Thy salvation and strengthen me with a perfect spirit."[33]

_____

33 - Ps. 50:12-14.

CHAPTER 6

VENIAL AND MORTAL SIN

S T. AMBROSE tells us that sin is the breaking of the
law of God, or disobedience to the divine commandments. In other words, there are two general classes of sin:
sin of commission, and sin of omission. Sins of commission
are like the performance of an evil deed, such as robbery
or murder. Since they consist in performing an act, anyone can recognize them. Now, sins of omission the failure to perform some prescribed good work, such as not
to fast or not to pray. Since these sins consist in the failure
to perform an act, men do not see them as clearly. For that
reason, some spiritual persons, especially if they are simple
people, often find no sins with which to accuse themselves
when examining their conscience. Since they do not fall
into many sins of commission, and they do not clearly see
their sins of omission, they find nothing to confess.

Sins are also divided according to how serious they are. Some are generally mortal sins, while others are generally venial sins, and lastly, some may be either venial or mortal. We must always be careful to guard ourselves against all sin of any kind, and especially against mortal sins. Recalling the theological virtues of faith, hope and charity, we remember that God infuses these in our soul. The virtues of faith and hope are only lost by sins which are committed directly against them, such as heresy and despair respectively. Yet with the virtue of charity, which is nothing other than the presence of sanctifying grace, the love of God in our souls, it is lost along with other infused virtues through the commission of a single mortal sin. This is because by such sins we oppose ourselves to the love of God, and by malice make our souls an unsuitable place for His indwelling grace.

Now, so that we might be able to distinguish between mortal and venial sins, two rules should be kept in mind. The first and general rule is that mortal sin is directly opposed to charity, and by charity we here understand the love of God and neighbor. Accordingly, anything contrary to the honor of God or the good of one's neighbor in a serious matter is a mortal sin. Such sins are called mortal because they kill the spiritual life.

The second rule is more particular and it states that anything contrary to the Commandments of God or the Church is a mortal sin. But it is to be noted that a sin which is generally mortal may become venial under certain circumstances, namely if through a lack of deliberation or full consent of the will the act is not fully mortal. In such instances that which in itself is mortally sinful is no more than a venial sin.

Venial sins receive their name from the Latin word *venia*, which means pardon. This is because they are more easily pardoned than mortal sins. Some persons commit venial sins in spite of their good resolutions, usually out of laziness or negligence or as the result of the remnants of evil habits that yet remain in the soul. Others have a lax conscience and do not make sufficient good resolutions. They are content merely to avoid mortal sin, and apart from that, they like to eat and drink excessively and waste much time in talk and in other pastimes to which generally there are many venial sins attached. Such persons will never receive pardon for these sins no matter how often they confess them, unless they make a true resolution to amend their lives. Otherwise they appear to have every intention of continuing to commit such sins. Such people live in constant danger because, as St. Thomas points out, anyone that does not have the firm determination to improve, is likely to become worse. A man who tries to remain stationary in the middle of a fast-flowing river will be carried away by the current. In the same way, he is in much danger of falling back in the spiritual life who does not strive to advance. However, those who commit venial sins through carelessness or negligence are more quickly converted and more easily obtain pardon, for it is not in man's power, however perfect he be, to avoid all venial sins. "A just man shall fall seven times and shall rise again;

but the wicked shall fall down into evil."[34] St. Augustine says that saintly men have reason to weep for their faults but in spite of this they are truly saints because they have a holy desire to do all that is required for perfect sanctity.

As to those sins that may be either venial or mortal, they are usually the more serious venial sins and very close to mortal sins. Some of these are called the deadly sins, because they lead to so many others, and they must be avoided with greatest diligence. Others are not classed in that number, but can quickly pass from venial to mortal.

The first is envy, for although it frequently concerns light matter and is more a movement of the passions than a deliberate act of the will, it militates against charity, which is the very life of the soul. Therefore, a man ought to flee from this sin as from death itself. The second sin is anger, and although in the majority of instances it is not a mortal sin, it is still serious, for it upsets the soul and disturbs peace of conscience. The third sin is criticism, which sometimes becomes detraction, which is to reveal true information that is detrimental to our neighbor when the other party has no right to it. It often happens that when one begins to criticize the public and known faults of another, he easily proceeds to reveal another's secret sins and thus blackens the reputation of his neighbor. The fourth sin is ridicule, or derision of one's neighbor, which has all the ugliness of the former sin but adds to it a certain pride, presumption, disdain, and contempt that are abominable to God and man.

---

34 - Prov. 24:16.

The fifth sin is rash judgment of one's neighbor, that is, interpreting as evil that which could as easily be interpreted as good. We see that if certain wealthy women lack something in their home or are jealous of their husbands, their sorrow or distrust gives rise to suspicions and they pass judgments on others, however light the reasons for so doing. Some men will see others who are more successful than they are, and become angry because they cannot see the reason for it. What is worse, both sometimes openly express what is in their heart and commit two sins: that of judging their neighbor and that of bearing false testimony. The sixth sin is lying and flattery, which may become mortal if it is a question of grave matter; moreover, if it is accompanied by damage to one's neighbor, there is an obligation to make restitution. Such are the sins into which people most frequently fall and we must avoid them as much as possible.

There are some who, when they fall into mortal sin, they decide to commit this sin again and again before going to confession. Take care that you do not become like this! Heed the words of the wise man who tells you that he who disdains the little things will soon fall in the great things. Although it is true that neither seven nor seven thousand venial sins make one mortal sin, St. Augustine warns us: "Do not underestimate venial sins because they are small, but fear them because they are so numerous." However small they may be, they do great damage to the soul. They weaken devotion, disturb peace of conscience, make the heart torpid, smother the fervor of charity, soften the rigor of the ascetical life, and offer resistance to the Holy Spirit. There is no enemy, however small, which, if we ignore it, cannot do us much harm.

Instead, let us take care to cleanse ourselves of the stains of venial sin, for St. John tells us that nothing stained can enter the heavenly Jerusalem. Therefore, if these stains are not purged in this life, they must be cleansed in the fires of purgatory which, although they are not eternal, are more painful than anything that we could suffer in this life.

The remedies against venial sin are the following: humble accusation of one's sins, fervent recitation of the Our Father, the use of bodily mortifications, and other pious practices. Every man must render an account on the day of judgment for every idle word. Job says: "I feared all my works, knowing that Thou didst not spare the offender."[35] And the Apostle tells us: "Therefore you are inexcusable, O man, whosoever you are that judges. For wherein you judge another, you condemn yourself. For you do the same things which you judge. For we know that the judgment of God is, according to truth, against them that do such things. And think on this, O man, that judges them who do such things, and do the same, that you shall escape the judgment of God? ... Do you not know that the mercy of God leads you to penance?"[36]

_____

35 - Job 9:28.

36 - Rom. 2:1-4.

We should notice, however, that there is a difference between imperfections and venial sins. Some things are imperfections but are not sins, as happens when one neglects to perform a good work that he could have performed, for we are not always obliged in each instance to perform the good work. One could give more alms than he does or pray more than he prays or fast more than he fasts, but to fail in such things is not always a sin. Rather, it may be only a weakness or imperfection. Nevertheless, the devout person does not fail to accuse himself of such things, because in so doing he humbles himself before the representative of Christ and endeavors to depart from his imperfections.

Now if we turn to a consideration of mortal sin, we must observe that there are two deformities in every mortal sin: the disordered love of some created thing, which moves us to sin, and a disregard for God's laws, which we despise when we sin. The second deformity is more serious than the first, as David admitted when he accused himself of his sin: "Against you alone have I sinned."[37] What could be more unworthy of the great majesty of God than to place before it something so lowly as a created good? How similar to the action of those who preferred Barabbas to Christ! What is this but to take from God the crown and glory that are due to Him and to attribute them to some created thing? For he who places any created thing higher than God, places his ultimate end in that creature.

---

37 - Ps. 50:6.

In order to avoid so great an evil, we should observe that a man descends to mortal sin by three steps: by suggestion, delight, and consent. By suggestion we mean that the world, the flesh, or the devil arouse in us some evil thought; by delight we mean the complacency and interest with which we receive the evil suggestion; by consent we mean that the will, moved by pleasure or the prospect of pleasure, deliberately consents to the evil. It is so important to understand this procession of evil, because anyone who wishes to avoid the last stages must also avoid the first inclinations. The first seed is the evil thought, which proceeds from the temptation, and if one uproots this seed from the first sprouts, all the branches and fruits that would have proceeded from it are likewise destroyed. Consequently, one of the principal counsels given to the Christian is that he should resist evil thoughts. But if he acts otherwise, he will offend God by dallying with the evil thought, and he will have to exert all the greater effort to rid himself of it if he has retained the thought for any length of time.

Although the Christian should carefully avoid all mortal sin, he should be especially careful of the following, for they are frequently committed. The first sin is blasphemy, which is closely related to the three worst sins: infidelity, despair, and direct hatred of God. We will find that weak souls who fall away from the faith may despair of being good, and as they embrace sins which are against God's law, they bear a hatred to God. Men today say that God does not want us to have any fun, and so hate him because

41

knowing their sin is against God's law impedes their enjoyment of them. On the other hand, Souls attempting to lead a spiritual life do not usually commit this sin, but they commit others that are very similar to it: they turn against God in the labors that He sends to them, they complain against Him and His providence, or they say that they do not like the kind of life He has bestowed on them.

The second sin, taking the name of the Lord in vain, is also directly against God and is for that reason more serious than sins committed against one's neighbor. It is true, however, that if a man does this through carelessness or without due consideration, he may be excused from mortal sin, for where there is no deliberation or full consent of the will, there is no serious sin. Yet if we find an abuse of the Lord's name routinely escapes our lips because it has become a habit, we must strive to do all we can to break the habit.

The third sin which the Christian should especially avoid is every kind of lust. A man can fall into sins of this type by thought, word, deed, desire, or morose delectation. Morose delectation occurs when a man deliberately takes pleasure in a lustful thought, even if he has no intention of performing the deed. This is as much a mortal sin as the others. The man in such a position realizes what he is thinking and wishes to retain that type of thought. However, if such thoughts come to mind spontaneously and the man does not realize what he is doing, but later recollects himself and endeavors to rid himself of such thoughts, he is not guilty of mortal sin, because of the lack of deliberation. Still we must be careful, because with some sins the devil fishes with a hook, but with sins of lust he brings a net. It is another cheat of this world that the sensible enjoyment which God gave as a reward for being a part of his creative plan is twisted to vain desires which lead to misery.

The fourth sin is that of hatred, and it is usually accompanied by desires for revenge. If the animosity or hatred between persons does not reach the point of a desire for revenge, it is not usually a mortal sin, but otherwise it is generally serious. It eats away at the charity we should have for our neighbor, and scandalizes our fellow Christians. A man caught in the grip of hatred will often, step by step, wound the indwelling presence of God in his soul and commit those acts which will cause it to depart completely.

The fifth sin is willful possession of property against the will of the rightful owner. As long as someone persists in holding on to someone else's property in this way, he is in the state of sin, just as he would be if he failed to remedy bad blood with another or were living in fornication. For it is not only a sin to take someone else's property, but also to retain it against his will. Having the intention of making restitution later on is not enough if he is able to make restitution at once, for such a person not only has the obligation to make restitution, but of doing so as soon as he can. If a man cannot make restitution at all or if he cannot do so without reducing himself to abject poverty, then there is no obligation to restitution at that time, because God does not demand the impossible.

The sixth sin is that of violating the precepts of the Church, which oblige under serious obligation. These are to attend Mass on Sundays and holy days, to confess once a year, to receive Holy Communion during the Easter season, and to fast or abstain on the days prescribed, as well as to provide for the upkeep of the ministers of the Church through tithes. In regard to attendance at Mass, it is true, of course, that if one is prevented by some urgent and reasonable necessity, no sin is committed, because necessity excuses from the law. This holds true for legitimate necessities in other Ecclesiastical precepts. Yet, we must be cautious on this point; are we really impeded? How many faithful are negligent in the matter of supporting their pastors? Oftentimes it is those who can most afford it who fail to give, while those who can least afford it are generous in offering the little they have, in the fashion of the widow in the Gospel who offered a paltry sum, but was praised by our Savior for how great a sacrifice it was.

Let us now consider the effects of mortal sin. First of all, the sinner loses the grace of the Holy Spirit, which is the greatest gift that God could give to any creature. The virtue of Charity also is lost, as well as all the infused virtues (except faith and hope) and the gifts of the Holy Spirit. The sinner is deprived of the right to the kingdom of heaven, for this right proceeds from the possession of grace, as St. Paul tells us when he says that glory is given through grace. Having lost the status of an adopted son of God, the sinner no longer enjoys the special care of divine providence which is given to the just. Moreover, the man in mortal sin loses the peace and serenity of a good conscience, the consolations of the Holy Spirit, and the merit of all the good works that he has performed throughout his life. He also loses the full participation in the goods of the Church, to the extent that he cannot share in them as completely as he did while in the state of grace.

All this is lost by a single mortal sin. And what does the sinner gain by his sin? As long as he remains in sin he is a condemned man, doomed to suffer the pains of hell for all eternity. His name is erased from the book of life. Instead of being a child of God, he has become a slave of the devil. But of all the losses, the greatest by far is that the sinner has lost God, and this is the root and cause of all the other evil effects of sin. To lose God is to cease to have Him as one's Father and Good Shepherd and to make of Him a severe judge and an enemy. Should not one weep if he has lost so great a good?

How ashamed will be the man that has the misfortune to fall into so many evils! O miserable soul, consider what you were and what you are now. Formerly you were a spouse of the Most High, a temple of the living God, a chosen vessel, and an heir to the kingdom of heaven. All this you once were, and as often as I say that you were once these things, you have reason to weep. What madness made you throw it all away? For the pleasure of a cruel word against your neighbor, for the fleeting delights of lust, for the conceit of making a little more money, you have lost everything!

What is the meaning of this great change? Why has the bride of God become an adulteress with Satan? Why has a temple of the Holy Spirit become a nest of vipers, the chosen vessel a cistern of corruption, and the companion of the saints a companion of devils? She who once flew through the heavens like a dove, now crawls upon the earth like a serpent.

Weep, then, poor, unfortunate soul, and free yourself from this sad condition. The angels weep for you, the heavens weep for you, and all the saints weep for you. The tears of St. Paul are shed for you because you have sinned and have not done penance. The prophets weep for you because they see that the fury of divine justice will descend upon you. For you, much more than for the fallen walls of Jerusalem, Jeremias weeps, because he sees that a daughter of Sion has lost her beauty.

No one can say in this life: "My heart is clean; I am free from sin." Therefore, it is well for us to know what are the remedies for sin. The first and principal remedy is the sacrament of reconciliation, without which a man in mortal sin has no other remedy. After baptism, this is the most important medicine that has been prescribed for us by the divine Physician. The second remedy is sorrow for sin, the sacrifice of a contrite heart which God never despises. Thus David tells us that God looks upon the hearts of the humble and does not despise their prayers and St. Augustine says that it is not enough to turn away from our sins, but that we must add to this the weeping of humility, the sorrow of penance, and the performance of works of mercy. The third remedy is the atonement for sin by almsgiving which, as Tobias tells us, frees a man from every sin and from death and does not allow him to pass into darkness. The fourth remedy is to seek pardon for our sins by forgiving our neighbors' offenses against us, for Christ tells us that if we forgive our neighbors, the heavenly Father will forgive us. The fifth remedy is to give spiritual help for the salvation of our neighbors, for St. James teaches that he who converts a sinner from his evil way delivers his own soul from death and covers a multitude of his own sins. The sixth remedy is humble prayer, similar to that of the man who prayed: "O God, be merciful to me, a sinner." The seventh and last remedy is the love of God, which cleanses the soul as fire cleanses iron of its rust. "Many sins are forgiven her because she has loved much."

CHAPTER 7

SINS AGAINST THE HOLY SPIRIT

THE SINS against the Holy Spirit are those grievous sins of which Christ said that they will not be forgiven either in this life or in the next. God will not give His grace to those who do not abhor sin and resolve to lead a good life, and this is the condition of those who commit sins against the Holy Spirit, for out of pure malice they reject the mercy and grace that the Holy Spirit offers.

A man can sin in three ways: through sloth, willful ignorance, or malice. To sin through sloth is to sin against the Father, to whom is attributed power, and in this way St. Peter sinned when he denied Christ.[38] To sin through willful ignorance is to sin against the Son, to whom wisdom is attributed, and in this way St. Paul sinned when he

---

38 - Matt. 26:25.

persecuted the Church.[39] To sin through malice is to sin against the Holy Spirit, to whom we attribute goodness, and in this way the Pharisees sinned.

Theologians enumerate six sins against the Holy Spirit: presumption, despair, resistance of a known truth, envy of another's spiritual good, obstinacy in evil, and final impenitence. Presumption is an excessive confidence in divine mercy to the extent that a man puts aside all fear of the Lord and abandons himself recklessly to every kind of sin. Such is the attitude of those who are so confident of divine mercy that they expect to reach heaven without performing any works of penance. They are totally unmindful of the words of the Apostle: "Do you think O man, … that you will escape the judgment of God? Or do you despise the riches of His goodness and patience and longsuffering? Do you not know that the mercy of God leads you to penance? But according to your hardness and impenitent heart, you treasure up for yourself wrath, against the day of wrath, and revelation of the just judgment of God."[40] Sirach also warns us against this sin in the following words: "Be not without fear about sin forgiven, and add not sin upon sin. And say not, 'The mercy of the Lord is great; He will have mercy on the multitude of my sins.' For mercy and wrath quickly come from Him, and His wrath looks upon sinners."[41]

---

39 - Cf. Gal. 1:13.

40 - Rom. 2:3-5.

41 - Sir. 5:7.

The second sin against the Holy Spirit is despair or lack of trust in divine mercy. This occurs when a man abandons all hope of obtaining pardon from God or of attaining eternal life. Cain sinned in this way when he said: "My iniquity is greater than that I may deserve pardon."[42] Judas also sinned in this way when he hanged himself. But we know that in this life it is never too late for repentance, as was manifested by the thief on the cross.

The third sin against the Holy Spirit is deliberate resistance of a known truth, not of any truth at all, but of a divine truth, with the result that the purity of faith is corrupted. In this way the Pharisees sinned, for they knowingly denied Christ even though they could not deny the truth of His miracles. The Psalmist refers to such sinners as those who sit "in the chair of pestilence;"[43] St. Peter calls them "lying teachers who bring in sects of perdition;"[44] and St. Paul says that they are heretics, corrupted in their intellects and reprobate in the faith, deceived by the spirit of error, and perverted and condemned by their own judgments.

The fourth sin against the Holy Spirit is envy of the spiritual goods of one's neighbor, and this occurs when a man is saddened at the virtues and gifts which God mercifully bestows upon another. This sin seems more proper to devils than to men, for Satan is exceedingly saddened

---

42 - Gen. 4:13.

43 - Ps. 1:1.

44 - 2 Pet. 2:1.

to see grace preserved and increased in us. Sadly, this sin can even be seen in monasteries.

The fifth sin against the Holy Spirit is obstinacy in evil and this takes place when a man clings so stubbornly to his evil ways that he cannot be made to depart from them. Such was the case with Pharaoh, who had so often been warned and punished by God but would not cease from his tyranny and died in his sin.[45] Such also are they of whom the Psalmist spoke when he said that they are "like the deaf asp that covers her ears, which will not hear the voice of the charmers," that is, the teaching of the Church.[46] They seem to say: "Depart from us; your way of thinking be far from us."[47]

The sixth sin against the Holy Spirit is that of final impenitence, which happens when a man does not wish to put an end to his sins but proposes never to do penance and never to be converted from his evil ways. The death of such sinners is described by the Psalmist as "very evil,"[48] for these men, although they may not say so in words, manifest by their deeds the words of Isaias: "We have entered into a league with death, and we have made a covenant with hell."[49] Such are the sins against the Holy Spirit and since they are more grievous than any others

---

45 – Exod. 5:6.

46 – Ps. 57:5.

47 – Job 22:17.

48 – Ps. 33:22.

49 – Isa. 28;15.

and are seldom pardoned, we must be sufficiently armed against them.

In addition to the sins against the Holy Spirit, there are others that cry to heaven for vengeance. The first is the sin of murder, which was the sin of Cain, to whom God said: "The voice of thy brother's blood cries to Me from the earth."[50] The second is the abominable sin of sodomy, of which God said: "The men of Sodom were very wicked, and sinners before the face of the Lord beyond measure."[51] And the angels said to Lot: "For we will destroy this place because their cry is grown loud before the Lord."[52]

The third sin is oppression of the poor, against which God spoke in Exodus: "You shall not disturb a stranger nor afflict him, for yourselves also were strangers in the land of Egypt. You shall not hurt a widow or an orphan. If you hurt them they will cry out to Me and I will hear their cry, and My rage shall be enkindled and I will strike you with the sword, and your wives shall be widows and your children fatherless."[53] Pharao and the Egyptians were afflicted with many plagues and afterward were drowned in the sea because they oppressed the children of Israel. Again, speaking through Isaiah, the Lord warned us: "Woe to them that make wicked laws, and when they write,

---

50 – Gen. 4:10.

51 – Gen. 13:13.

52 – Gen. 19:13.

53 – Exod. 22:21-24.

write in justice to oppress the poor in judgment and do violence to the cause of the humble of My people, that widows might be their prey and that they might rob the fatherless."[54]

The fourth sin that cries to heaven for vengeance is to defraud laborers of their wages. St. James says of this sin: "Behold the hire of the laborers who have reaped down your fields, which by fraud has been kept back by you, cries, and the cry of them hath entered into the ears of the Lord of Sabaoth."[55] No less strong are the words of Sirach: "The bread of the needy is the life of the poor; he that defrauds them thereof is a man of blood. He that takes away the bread gotten by sweat, is like him that kills his neighbor."[56] In addition to this, the divine law commands us: "You will not refuse the hire of the needy and the poor, whether he be your brother or a stranger that dwelleth with thee in the land and is within your gates. But you shall pay him the price of his labor the same day, before the going down of the sun, because he is poor, and with it maintains his life, lest he cry against you to the Lord and it be reputed to you for a sin."[57]

These four sins are enumerated in Scripture so that we may know how grievous they are and how severely they will be punished by God, both in this life and in the

---

54 – Isa. 1–2.

55 – Jas. 5:4.

56 – Sirach 34:25–26.

57 – Deut. 24:14–15.

next. The fruit that we gain from a consideration of this doctrine is that we learn the gravity of sins and we are urged to avoid grave sin with greater fear and to repent with greater sorrow of any fault we may have incurred in these matters. We also learn what a great difference there is between the wise man and the fool, the just man and the sinner, according to the words of Solomon: "A wise man feareth and declineth from evil; the fool leapeth over and is confident."[58]

---

58 – Prov. 14:16.

CHAPTER 8

THE SLAVERY OF SIN

"AMEN, amen I say to you, that whosoever sins is the servant of sin. Now the servant does not abide in the house forever, but the Son abides forever. If, therefore, the Son shall make you free, you shall be free indeed."[59] In these words the Lord gives us to understand that there are two types of liberty. One which has the appearance of liberty but in reality is false, and the other which is true liberty. That is a false liberty wherein the body is free but the soul is held captive by being subject to the tyranny of sin and passion. True liberty, on the other hand, is that in which the soul is free of all tyranny, whether the body be free or not.

The reason why we call liberty of soul a true liberty is because the soul is incomparably more noble than the

---

59 - John 8:34–36.

body. For that reason, he is truly free who enjoys liberty of soul, but he enjoys only apparent freedom whose soul is enslaved while his body has complete liberty of action. And if you ask me to whom such a man is enslaved, I shall answer that he is a slave of the most base and despicable tyrant that can be imagined—sin. The truth of this statement is borne out by the words of our Lord: "Whosoever commits sin is the servant of sin."[60]

But the sinner is not only the slave of sin, but also the slave of the principal instigators of sin: the world, the flesh, and the devil. Any servant of the son is likewise a servant of the parents, and these three things are the parents of sin. This is why they are called enemies of the soul, because once they gain dominion over the soul, they subject it to the tyranny of sin. Yet there is this difference among them: the world and the devil cater to the flesh, in much the same way that Eve persuaded Adam and led him to sin. Hence, St. Paul designates the flesh as sin. However, we commonly refer to the flesh as sensuality or concupiscence, to signify the disordered sensitive appetites or passions which incline us to sin.

An excessive attraction for the things that we desire makes us strive to obtain them at any cost and to overcome every obstacle that lies in our path, even when the thing desired is forbidden by the law of God. This is why St. Basil advises that the principal weapon against sin is holy desires. It is evident from this that the sensitive

---

60 - John 8:34.

appetite is one of the principal tyrants to which evil men are enslaved when, as the Apostle says, they are "sold under sin."[61] St. Paul does not mean that the sinner loses his free will through sin, for he will never lose that, however many sins he may commit, but that the sinner's free will becomes so flaccid and his passions become so strong that the sinner is under the sway of his sensitive appetite.

If you wish to understand something of the power and tyranny of the passions, consider the evils they have caused and still cause in the world. Consider what adulterers will do to satisfy their disordered passion. They know full well that if their spouse should find out, they would suffer shame, dishonor, scandalize their families, and lose their souls. Nevertheless, so great is the power of passion that it makes them ignore all these evils and drink eagerly of the horrible cup of sin. What other tyrant has ever commanded that a slave obey him under the risk of losing so much? What slavery could be more demanding and rigorous than this? They who suffer under the tyranny of this vice can scarcely be called their own masters, and neither the fear of God, of death, of hell, nor the possible loss of life, honor, and heaven itself deter them from their evil way nor enable them to break the chains of their captivity.

What shall I say of the jealousy, fear, suspicions, dread, and dangers in which such persons live day and night, risking life and soul for sensual pleasures? Does any tyrant in the whole world have such power over the body of his

---

61 - Cf. Rom. 7:14.

slaves as this appetite does over the human heart? No servant is so bound to his master that he does not have some moments in which he may rest from his duties, but this vice and others like it are such that once they have gained control of the heart, a man scarcely has time for anything else.

Just the same, tyranny is not found in this vice alone, rather, it is common to many others as well. If you do not think so, consider the vainglorious and ambitious man. See how he lives, a slave to his ambition. Everything in his life is directed to this one end. Whatever he does, he does so that he will make the best appearance and be praised and admired. Whatever he does becomes a net or snare to capture the applause of men and gain popularity.

Who is more foolish than the wretched man who spends his whole life seeking the smoke and air of glory and praise? He cannot do as he pleases, cannot dress as he pleases, and cannot go where he pleases. Sometimes he does not even go to church or speak with good people, for fear of what the world will say. What is equally as bad, he is forced to spend much more than he wishes and even more than he can afford.

And what shall I say of the miser, who is not only a slave of money but an idolater, for he worships and obeys its every command. For the sake of money he will fast and even take the bread from his own mouth. He loves money more than he loves his God and as a result, he sins against God time and time again for the sake of money. For the sake of his money he will not pay his employees well, or will compel them to work on feast days. He will not give alms to the poor, lest his worship of Mammon be diminished. Money is his rest, his glory, his hope. His heart and mind are so fixed on wealth that he is forgetful of self and everyone else. Is such a man the master of his own wealth and able to do with it as he wishes? Or is he not the slave and captive of money? The avaricious man does not use money; money uses him.

What greater slavery than slavery to our own passions? You call him a prisoner who is confined behind bars or whose hands and feet are bound; how is he not also a prisoner whose soul is shackled by the disorderly affection for some created good? When this happens, there is no faculty in a man that remains perfectly free. He is no longer master of himself, but a slave of that which he loves, for whatever he loves, holds his heart captive. And it matters not what kind of bonds hold him prisoner if the best part of a man is thus enslaved.

It also does not lessen the slavery if a man freely chooses to be a captive, rather, it will be all the more dangerous as it is voluntary. And there is no greater slavery than for a man to be so captivated by the object of his passion as to close his eyes to God, truth, honesty, and the laws of justice. The drunkard is not master of himself, rather, alcohol rules him; the avaricious man is not master of himself, but the servant of money. And if the slavery itself is a torment, consider the misery that these wretched men suffer when they cannot achieve that which they desire and yet cannot cease to desire it, so that they know not what to do or which way to turn. Such men must say to their ruling passion: "I love you and I hate you, because I cannot live with you nor can I live without you."

If these were the only shackles or bonds, the sinner's lot would not be so wretched, for if a man is attacked by only one enemy, he is less likely to despair of victory. But what of the many other bonds that hold the sinner a prisoner? Some men are so afraid that they cannot extricate themselves from any difficulty or evil. Others are melancholy and as a result, they also may become fearful or even vehement. Still others are timid and everything appears great to them and worthy of great esteem, because to the small heart everything appears great. Others are naturally vehement in all their desires, as is frequently the case with women, of whom the Philosopher says that they either love or they hate because they do not know how to moderate their affections.

All these persons suffer to some extent from the tyranny of their passions and if it is a lamentable state to be bound by one chain and to be the slave of one master, what must it be to be bound with so many chains and to be a slave of so many masters? If man's dignity rests on his reason and free will, what can be more contrary to these two faculties than the passions? Passion blinds reason and takes the will captive. From all this you can see the danger and harm of any disordered passion, for it drags a man down from the throne of his dignity, it obscures his reason and perverts his free will, so that a man is no longer a man but a beast. Such is the wretched slavery of those who are not ruled by God or reason but by their passions.

CHAPTER 9

MANUAL FOR AVOIDING SIN

NOW that we have seen the various types of sin and the means by which we may purge ourselves of sin, let us consider the ways in which we can protect ourselves against sin. The first safeguard is to arouse in our hearts the firm resolution to die rather than commit a serious sin. Just as a virtuous wife is prepared to die rather than betray her husband, so the Christian should be so loyal to God that he would endure any hardship rather than betray his God. So, to enkindle in your heart this holy resolve, it will be of great help to recall what a man loses through mortal sin. When you see that the evil effects of sin are so numerous and so serious, you will be amazed that certain men can fall into serious sin so easily.

In the first place, mortal sin deprives a man of the grace of God, which is His greatest gift to us. For grace is a supernatural quality which enables man to participate in the divine nature and which makes him God, so to speak. Mortal sin also destroys man's friendship with God, and if it is a great loss to be deprived of the friendship of the great ones of this world, how much greater to lose that of the King of heaven and earth? Lastly, serious sin causes the loss of the infused virtues and the gifts of the Holy Spirit, which adorn and beautify the soul of the just and fortify it against the power of Satan.

Moreover, the sinner is deprived of the right to the kingdom of heaven, which is an effect of sanctifying grace, for St. Paul tells us that grace gives life everlasting.[62] He loses the spirit of adoption which makes him a child of God and bestows on him the fatherly providence which God manifests to those whom He receives as His sons. The prophet rejoiced in this adoption when he said: "Because Thou hast been my helper and I will rejoice under the covert of Thy wings."[63] He loses the peace and serenity of a good conscience and the consolations of the Holy Spirit, which incomparably surpass all the riches and delights of this world. He loses the merit of all the good works he has ever performed, as well as his participation and communication in the goods of Christ, for the sinner is no longer united to Christ through grace.

The sinner's condition is like that of Samson after he had lost his hair, the source of his strength. In his weakened

---

62 – Rom. 6:22.

63 – Ps. 62:8.

condition he was at the mercy of his captors, who bound him hand and foot, gouged out his eyes, tied him to the turnstile of a mill, and made him grind grain like an animal.[64] In like manner, the sinner who has lost sanctifying grace is too weak to resist evil inclinations; he is bound hand and foot so that he cannot perform good works; he is blinded to the knowledge of divine things; he is a captive of the devils and occupies himself with the things of an animal by seeking to satisfy the demands of his passions.

Is not this a condition greatly to be feared? Do you not think that these losses should be avoided at any cost? How can men who dare to commit such sins be considered reasonable? Truly, mortal sin is so horrible a thing that the sight of it would cause more terror in us than the sight of hell itself. And it is even worse when we consider how much God hates it, the fearful punishment that He has prepared for it, and all that He did and suffered to destroy it.

Therefore, arouse in your heart the firm resolution never to sin and if at any time you are tempted to do so, place on one side of the balance all the losses we have mentioned and on the other side, the advantage and delight of sin. Then decide whether it is reasonable that you should surrender such precious treasures for some temporal pleasure or gain, as Esau did when he sold his birthright for a mess of pottage and surrendered the paternal blessing.[65]

---

64 - Judg. 16:21.

65 - Gen. 25:34.

Secondly, if you wish to avoid sin you must avoid the occasions of sin, otherwise you will be lamented as one already dead. If you are not sailing to a certain harbor, why are you on the boat? If a man should be so weak that he frequently falls to the ground, what assurance will he have that he will not fall if someone pulls him by the arm or gives him a blow? Likewise, if a man is so weakened as a result of his sins that he falls many times without provocation, what will he do when he is faced with temptations and occasions of sin? The occasion of sin is like the gateway. In and of itself it is not sinful. It is rather the moment where one knows that he is more inclined toward an act than when he is elsewhere. A man who struggles with drunkenness will put himself in the occasion of sin by going to a tavern. Or again, a man who struggles with fornication and adultery will not sin by going near a place where women of ill-repute happen to be; rather it is the gateway to committing those sins.

The third protection against sin is to resist temptation at the very beginning. To do this, one should recall the figure of Christ crucified, covered with wounds and flowing rivers of blood, and realize that He was brought to that condition because of sin. Then the sinner will tremble at the thought of being partly responsible for placing God in such a state. Considering these things, he will call upon God from the depths of his heart, asking to be delivered from temptation so that His great sufferings will not have been in vain. This requires an act of the will to overcome our passions which are inflamed on account of temptation.

Whether it is the desire for the thing, or the fear of missing a delight, the temptation must be defeated and so that we can embrace Christ on the cross as our brother.

The fourth safeguard against sin is the reception of the sacraments, which were instituted by Christ to purge us of our past sins and to preserve us from future sins. And although the worthy reception of the sacraments is of great spiritual benefit at all times, this is especially true in times of temptation. Moreover, of all the sacraments, the sacrament of penance is the one principal remedy for ridding ourselves of sin. If you should fall into sin, on no account go to your bed that night with the sin on your soul, for you know not whether you will rise from that bed on the morrow. Endeavor to confess your sin on that very day and to repent of it, for St. Gregory says that if we do not rid ourselves of our sins, they will bring other sins in their wake. But what if someone lives very far from a Church? What remedy will he seek? An act of perfect contrition, made with sorrow for your sins for God's sake, not from the fear of hell.

The fifth remedy against sin is the practice of examining our conscience each night before we go to bed to account for the deeds done that day. Considering the various types of sin and the chief remedies against sin, you can discover whether you must accuse yourself before God of pride and vainglory; of envy, hatred, and enmities; of suspicions and rash judgments; of false vanity concerning the goods of this world; of disordered desires for worldly possessions or honors; of temptations against faith or chastity;

of lies, idle speech, or unnecessary swearing; of ridicule and unkind words against your neighbor; of slothfulness and negligence in the works of virtue; of lukewarmness in the love of God, ingratitude to Him, and forgetfulness of the blessings received from Him; of aridity in prayer and lack of charity for the poor. Then repent of all your faults and ask forgiveness of the Lord, firmly resolving to amend your life. And after you have washed your bed with tears, as David advises,[66] you will notice a great relief of conscience and will sleep peacefully.

Anyone who is frequently tempted in regard to some particular vice should, in addition to this nightly examination of conscience and act of contrition, arm themselves each morning with good resolutions and prayers against this vice, seeking special help from God. This practice will truly help the soul in conquering the enemy. It is also helpful to devote yourself to some special goal, such as the destruction of a particular vice or the cultivation of some virtue, for in this way the soul gradually makes progress in the spiritual life.

Another remedy against sin is the practice of frequent prayer, wherein we ask God for strength and grace and receive the consolations of the Holy Spirit, which make us lose our taste for the delights of this world and foster the spirit of devotion to make us prompt in the performance of virtuous deeds. Closely connected with this is the reading of good books, whereby time is well spent, the

---

66 – Ps. 67.

understanding is enlightened with the knowledge of truth, and the will is aroused to devotion, with the result that we are better fortified against sin and more inclined to virtue.

The Christian who engages in pious works and holy exercises is also protected against sin, for the idle man is like a fallow field which produces nothing but thorns and weeds. For this reason it is said that idleness teaches a man many evils.[67] But among the holy exercises that serve as a safeguard against sin, fasting, abstinence, and corporal penances are of special value. If the body is weakened through fasting and mortification, its passions and evil inclinations are likewise weakened. Therefore, it is a salutary counsel that the Christian should strive, especially on Fridays, to do some form of penance, however small, for this will serve not only as a protection against sin, but also as satisfaction for sin and an imitation of the sufferings of Christ.

Yet another remedy against sin is silence and recollection, for Solomon says that in a multitude of words, sin is not lacking.[68] We also read in the Imitation of Christ: "I never enter into the company of men that I do not depart less a man." Therefore, he who wishes to defend himself against sin should avoid useless conversations and frivolous association with others. Experience will soon teach him that if he does not do this, he will return home disconsolate and discontented, with his head filled with images that will make him wish he could recapture the time that has been wasted.

---

67 – Sirach. 37.

68 – Prov. 10:19.

The last two safeguards against sin are to strive conscientiously to avoid venial sin and to detach oneself from the world and its vanities. We have already seen that venial sins frequently lead to mortal sins, but the man that flees from even the smallest evil will be much better protected against the great evils. In regard to detachment from the world, St. James tells us that this is the first lesson that the Christian must learn if he wishes to be a friend of God: "Whosoever therefore will be a friend of this world becomes an enemy of God."[69] Moreover, Christ Himself has told us that we cannot serve two masters,[70] especially when they are so opposed to each other, for God is the sum of all good and this world is, as St. John says, "seated in wickedness."[71] You can be certain that he who does not break with this world, will commit many sins out of respect for the world or will neglect many obligations for the same reason. He will become a slave of the world and not a servant of God and rather than displease the world, he will choose to displease God.

In the battle against sin we do not so much need strong arms to fight nor feet to flee as we need eyes to see, for they are the principal weapons in our spiritual struggle.

The great concern of our adversary is so to disguise temptation that it does not appear as a temptation, but as something very reasonable. Thus, if he wishes to tempt

---

69 – Jas. 4:4.

70 – Matt. 6:24.

71 – 1 John 5:19.

us to pride or wrath or avarice he tries to make it appear reasonable for us to desire this honor, that wealth, or that vengeance. By making it appear that it would be contrary to reason to act otherwise, he hopes to deceive even those who are usually governed by reason. For that reason, the Christian must have eyes to see the hook that is hidden in the bait. The Christian must also have eyes to see the evil, degradation, danger, and harm that follow in the wake of the vice to which he is tempted. This will greatly assist him to control his passions and to refuse to taste that which, once having been tasted, leads to death. Truly, the servant of God must be all eyes, that is, he must have the foresight to make prudent investigations and judgments if he wishes to overcome vice and safeguard virtue.

CHAPTER 10

GOD'S LAW

IN TRACING out our quest for happiness, we have seen so much of what we must avoid if we wish to be truly happy. For the modern thinker, he will say that this is all to take away our earthly pleasure! What possible happiness is there in that! And if we stopped here, there would be some justice in the complaint. Nevertheless, in looking to the unhappiness of this world, its cheats, and the many deadly vices that assault us on our path, we are only preparing the ground for how it is we obtain true happiness. Just as the great preachers will warn, with great severity, those in the pew with the fear of damnation, and then turn to the happiness of heaven and the love of God, so we too shall now approach the goal of our Quest: True happiness.

For a good and happy life, knowledge and power are the two necessary things. In other words, we must know

what we ought to do to live a good life and we must have
the power to put this knowledge into practice through
our works. The first thing pertains to the law and the second pertains to grace, for the law gives us a knowledge of
good and evil, and grace gives us the power to do good
and avoid evil. The law illumines the intellect and grace
moves the will; the law teaches us the way to heaven, but
grace gives us the power to travel toward heaven. The law
is the body, but grace is the soul that gives life to the body.
God gave us the law through the hands of Moses, but He
gives us grace through His only-begotten Son, As St. John
says, "For the law was given by Moses; grace and truth
came by Jesus Christ."[72]

We hold it to be infallibly true, as declared and verified in Scripture, that God Himself is the Author of the
Ten Commandments. We read in Exodus: "And the Lord,
when He had ended these words in Mount Sinai, gave to
Moses two stone tablets of testimony, written with the
finger of God."[73] But if God is the Author of the law, it is
only fitting that we should hold it in the greatest honor
and reverence. For if the laws of a king, who is a mere
man, are honored and fulfilled, how much more should
one venerate and obey the law of God?

First of all, God's law teaches us what is and is not a
sin so that we shall always know when, in what manner,
and how seriously we sin. Thus, St. Paul tells us: "By the

---

72 - John 1:17.

73 - Exod. 31:18.

law is the knowledge of sin,"[74] and: "I do not know sin, but by the law."[75] This knowledge is a great incentive for us to seek the grace of God and to do penance for our sins.

Secondly, the law instructs us concerning good works and tells us what God wishes us to do in order to fulfill His holy will. St. Paul says: "The law indeed is holy, and the commandment holy and just and good."[76] The law enables us to know whether we are doing the will of the heavenly Father and whether we are moved by His Spirit in all that we do, for St. Paul says: "They who are in the flesh cannot please God."[77] Thus, the law is a spiritual sanction that commands us not to do evil but to live virtuously. "Why then was the law?" asks St. Paul; and he answers: "It was set because of transgressions."[78]

However, it may be asked: "What do Christians have to do with the Ten Commandments which were given to the Jews? We are not Jews; we are Christians, redeemed by the grace of Christ, as St. Paul tells us: 'You are not under the law, but under grace.'"[79]

We may answer this objection by saying that while it is true that the doctrine of Christ pertains to Christians, it is likewise certain that His doctrine is the perfection and

---

74 – Rom. 3:20.

75 – *Ibid.*, 7:7.

76 – *Ibid.*, 7:12.

77 – *Ibid.*, 8:8.

78 – Gal. 3:19.

79 – Rom. 6:14.

culmination of the Commandments of the law, as is stated in the fifth chapter of St. Matthew's Gospel. It follows, therefore, that the law of the Ten Commandments pertains no less to us Christians than to the Jews to whom it was first announced. Granted that Christ has freed us from the law, it does not follow that we are exempt from observing the Ten Commandments, for Christ freed us only from those laws that regulated the ceremonies, court procedures, and other affairs of the Jewish people. These statutes do not oblige us, because they were given only to the Jews and were to remain in force until the Messiah should come. But Christ did not liberate us from the fulfillment of the Ten Commandments; rather, He declared explicitly: "Do not think that I am come to destroy the law or the prophets. I am not come to destroy, but to fulfill. For amen I say to you, till heaven and earth pass, one jot or one tittle shall not pass of the law, till all be fulfilled. He that breaks one of these least commandments, and will teach men so, will be called the least in the kingdom of heaven. But he that will do and teach, he will be called great in the kingdom of heaven."[80]

The purpose of the commandments is that man should serve the Lord in all his actions, both internal and external. The will of God is declared through the Ten Commandments because these laws cover all the works in which a man may occupy himself in this life.

It is also to be noted that some of the Commandments command us to perform some specific work, such

---

80 - Matt. 5:17-18.

as to honor our father and mother. Others forbid certain actions, such as murder or theft. The obligations that flow from these two types of laws are also different. The precepts that place an obligation on us, do not do so in every circumstance. Thus, the Commandment that obligates us to honor our parents, requires the actual fulfillment only when the occasion arises.

Conversely, those precepts that forbid something are always obligatory, and in every circumstance. We are always forbidden to murder, to steal, or to hold the possessions of another against his will. This is why someone that has the goods of another does not fulfill the Commandment merely by having the intention of making restitution if he is actually able to make restitution here and now.

We should also understand that although some Commandments command a thing to be done and others forbid it, every the latter implies a positive one, and vice versa. For example, the Commandment to honor one's parents implies the that the opposite, to dishonor or injure them or to treat them with disrespect, is altogether forbidden. On the other hand, the Commandment which forbids us to have strange gods, implies the precept that commands us to acknowledge the true God and to adore and serve Him as such. These various aspects of the Commandments should always be borne in mind so that we shall the better understand them, and through understanding them may more easily obey them.

CHAPTER 11

DIVINE GRACE

FROM the two elements necessary for a good life—law and grace—the second element is much more necessary and excellent, just as the spirit is more excellent and necessary than the body and the New Testament is more excellent than the Old. The reason for this is that if men sin, it is not because of lack of knowledge of what is good and what is evil, for the natural light of reason suffices for this, but because of the corruption of the appetites, which often reject the good and seek evil. St. Paul speaks about this when he says: "For I do not that good which I will; but the evil which I hate, that I do."[81] In other words, man delights in the attraction and sweetness of vice but is repelled by the bitterness that he sees in virtue, although

---

81 - Rom. 7:15.

the latter is more salutary and profitable. Indeed, men have much greater need of the power to do good deeds than the ability to know good things, for all men to some degree know what is good, but not all men seek the good, due to the difficulties connected with it.

In this regard the sinner is in much the same state as a sick man, whose suffers such a loss of taste that he has no desire for the foods that will help him. When he is told to eat food that will do him good, he refuses to eat. Yet, this is not because he doesn't agree that the food is good for him, but because he has no appetite.

The sinner finds himself in a similar state because of his sin. The unfortunate man knows very well that his salvation depends on the observance of the Commandments of God, but he says that he does not feel drawn to these things. He realizes that charity, chastity, humility, patience, temperance, and the other virtues are the very health of his soul, but he despises these virtues and loves dishonesty, vanity, gluttony, licentiousness, and other vices. He simply has no appetite for virtue.

But if virtue is so natural to man, why is it that he finds its practice so difficult? If man is a rational animal and virtue is in conformity with reason, why does the rational creature find it so tedious to live and act in conformity with reason? With ease the horse runs, the birds fly, the fish to swim because all of these things are so conformable to the natures of these various animals. So if it is so much in conformity with the nature of the rational animal to live according to reason, why is it so difficult to do so?

If human nature were in that state of integrity in which God first created it, it would be very easy, to practice virtue. But man has fallen from that happy state because of Original Sin. Mankind has become sick, and it should come as no surprise that a sick man cannot do what a healthy man can do with ease. A healthy man can run and jump and do any number of things without much effort; but a sick man can hardly do these things if at all. When we look again to the state of man, no wonder that virtue is difficult and insipid to a man in a weakened state, whereas if he were spiritually strong and healthy, virtue would seem easy and perfectly conformable to nature.

It should be clear from this that the curses which God placed on our first parents because of their sin have affected them both spiritually and bodily. God told Eve that from now on she would bring forth her children in pain, whereas she had never previously known pain. So also, if it had not been for sin, man would have performed good works happily and with the greatest ease. Sadly, now because of sin the performance of good works is difficult for us because sin has debased our nature. Moreover, God said to Adam: "In the sweat of your face you shall eat bread,"[82] and this is also verified in the spiritual order, for we see with what sweat and labor man performs the works of the virtues, which are the true nourishment of our souls.

Again, we can apply to our flesh the curse that God placed upon the earth, of which He said that it would

---

82 - Gen. 3:19.

produce thorns and thistles. What land is there that produces as many thorns as our flesh? And if you want to know what these thorns are, listen to St. Paul: "Now the works of the flesh are manifest, which are fornication, uncleanness, immodesty, lust, idolatry, witchcrafts, enmities, contentions, emulations, wraths, quarrels, dissensions, sects, envies, murders, drunkenness, reveling, and such like."[83] The Apostle calls such things the works of the flesh because the root of all of them is our flesh corrupted by sin.

Such is the fruit that our flesh brings to harvest! If it is to produce any other fruit, it must be done by efforts, labor, and the sweat of our brow. The land that lies fallow produces, without effort or the help of anyone, clumps of thorns and thistles and other useless weeds. If one is to produce fruitful plants and healthy crops, the worker must plough the land, sow the seed, and cultivate the soil. In the same way, the land of our flesh will of itself produce the thorns of the vices and disordered appetites, and if it is to produce the flowers and fruits of the virtues, it requires much labor, industry, diligence, and the help of heaven. This, in addition to the effects of evil habits which intensify their natural depravity, is the reason men find it difficult to practice virtue.

Now you will ask: "If this is true, how are we to overcome such difficulties?" The same question was asked by the Apostle concerning the rebellion of the flesh: "Unhappy man that I am, who shall deliver me from the

---

83 - Gal. 5:19-21.

body of this death?"And he answered:"The grace of God, by Jesus Christ, our Lord."[84]

For this did Jesus come into the world: to reform our nature, to heal our wounds, and to be our Redeemer and Savior. What we have lost through the sin of the first Adam, we can regain through the grace of the second Adam. As the first Adam, by his pride and disobedience, has wounded our nature, the second Adam, by His humility and obedience, has given a remedy for these wounds: the grace of His passion. This grace reforms our nature, restores the image of God to our souls, makes the soul pleasing in the sight of God, and, by the virtues and holy habits that it produces, cures our evils, heals our wounds, enlightens our intellect, inflames our will, strengthens our weakness, pacifies our passions, rectifies our evil inclinations, restores our taste for spiritual things, gives us a distaste for earthly things, and makes the yoke of God's law sweet.

Jesus merited for us the first grace of conversion and justification, so that we are justified and are accepted by God as His children and heirs of His kingdom. After this first grace, Jesus merited for us all the other graces necessary for our salvation and to such an extent that the Eternal Father has never given and never will give any degree of grace except through the merits of the passion of His only-begotten Son. Moreover, a diversity of graces is communicated through the seven sacraments of the New Law,

---

84 - Rom. 7:24-25.

and although they have diverse effects according to the various needs of our souls, they all concur in the one common effect of bestowing grace on him who places no obstacles to its reception.

One of the principal means for obtaining grace is to plead for it from Him who alone can give it, for the Apostle tells us that the Lord is rich for all those who call upon Him. And what other virtue is required for this but the practice of prayer? "Ask, and it shall be given you; seek, and you shall find; knock, and it shall be opened to you."[85] What could be more generous on the part of God and of greater consolation to man? As St. John Chrysostom says, God will not deny assistance to those who ask for it is He that inspires us to ask.

And if you ask me what grace is, I shall tell you, in the language of theology, that grace is a participation in the divine nature. In other words, it is a sharing in the sanctity, goodness, purity, and nobility of God Himself, through which man casts off the baseness and villainy that is his by reason of his heritage from Adam and becomes a sharer in the divine perfection of Christ. To explain man's transformation through grace, the saints and holy writers are accustomed to use the example of iron cast into the fire. Without ceasing to be iron, it comes out of the fire entirely inflamed, possessing the brilliance, heat, and other characteristics of fire. In like manner, the heavenly quality of grace, when infused by God into the soul, has the

85 – Matt. 7:7.

marvelous power of transforming man into God, in such wise that without ceasing to be a man, he shares, according to his capacity, in the nature and life of God. As St. Paul says: "I live, now not I, but Christ lives in me."[86]

Grace is a supernatural and divine assistance which makes man live a life that is likewise supernatural and divine. In this the providence of God remarkably shines forth, for since He has willed that man should live two lives, one natural and the other supernatural, He has provided two forms or principles which are like two souls, one for the natural life and the other for the supernatural life. And just as the faculties and powers of the soul proceed from the essence of the soul, so also from the essence of grace, the soul of the spiritual life, proceed the infused virtues and the gifts of the Holy Spirit which perfect the various powers of the soul and facilitate them for the performance of good works. This will be greater in some souls than in others, depending on the degree of grace that is communicated to each soul.

Grace is a spiritual adornment which makes the soul so pleasing and beautiful in God's sight that He accepts the soul as His daughter and bride. In this way, the prophet rejoiced in the clothing of grace when he declared: "I will greatly rejoice in the Lord and my soul shall be joyful in my God, for He hath clothed me with the ornaments of salvation, and with the robe of justice He hath covered me, as a bridegroom decked with a crown and as a bride

---

86 - Gal. 2:20.

adorned with her jewels."[87] Grace is the vesture of many colors in which the daughter of the King is clothed as she sits at the right hand of her Spouse,[88] because from grace proceed the colors of all the virtues which beautify the just soul.

From what has been said, one can readily understand the effects that grace will produce in the soul. Its principal effect is that it makes the soul beautiful and pleasing in the sight of God so that He accepts it as His bride, His daughter, His temple, and His dwelling place. Here it is that He finds His delight among the children of men.

What picture could be more beautiful than this? If the beauty of the purely natural virtues is such that it captures the heart, what must be the beauty of a soul that is filled with grace and adorned with the riches of the supernatural virtues and the gifts of the Holy Spirit? There is no comparison whatever between the two kinds of beauty, because there is such a difference between God and man that there is no comparison between that which God effects and that which man accomplishes by his own efforts. God showed St. Catherine of Siena the vision of a soul in grace and when she was so overwhelmed by its beauty, and said to her: "See whether I was well employed in all that I suffered to beautify souls in this manner."

Another effect of grace is that it fortifies and strengthens the soul through the virtues that proceed from it.

---

87 – Isa. 61:10.

88 – Ps. 44:10.

These virtues are comparable to the hairs in which Samson found his beauty and his strength. Thus, the beauty and strength of the just soul are praised in the Song of Songs: "Who is she that comes forth as the morning rising, fair as the moon, bright as the sun, terrible as an army set in array?"[89] So great is the strength of the just soul that St. Thomas says that the slightest degree of grace suffices to overcome all the temptations and devils in the world.

Grace also makes a man so pleasing in God's sight that all the deliberate good actions performed by the just soul for supernatural motives are pleasing to God and meritorious of an increase of grace. As a result, not only strictly virtuous acts, but even natural actions such as eating and drinking and resting can be pleasing to God and meritorious, because if the one who performs these actions is pleasing to God, all his good works are likewise pleasing to God.

Moreover, grace makes man a son of God by adoption and an heir of the kingdom of heaven. It places his name in the book of life, where the names of all the just are written. Form this he acquires a right to the heritage of heaven, and this is the great privilege that the Savior commended so highly to His disciples when, they were pleased by the fact that even the devils obeyed their commands: "Rejoice not in this, that spirits are subject unto you, but rejoice in this, that your names are written in heaven."[90]

---

89 - Song 6:9.

90 - Luke 10:20.

To all these benefits we may add yet another marvelous effect of grace: the abiding presence of the Holy Spirit and of the entire Trinity in the souls of the just. The Savior tells us that a multitude of evil spirits makes the soul of the sinner their dwelling place, but once those infernal monsters are cast out, the Holy Spirit and the entire Trinity enter in and make it Their temple and dwelling place. As Christ says: "If anyone love Me, he will keep My word, and My Father will love him, and We will come to him and will make Our abode with him."[91]

By virtue of these words, all the holy doctors and theologians teach that the Holy Spirit, by some special manner of appropriation, dwells in the souls of the just. They make a distinction between the Holy Spirit and the gifts of the Holy Spirit, saying that not only are the gifts of the Holy Spirit received, but that the Holy Spirit Himself enters the soul and makes it His temple and dwelling place. He sanctifies and purifies the soul and adorns it with His gifts so that it will be a fitting abode for such a Guest. But the works of the Holy Spirit do not stop here. Not content with assisting us to enter into the gate of justice, He also aids us after we have entered into it so that we may walk along its paths, until He has led us, safe and secure, to the portal of salvation. For once the Holy Spirit has entered the soul through grace, He does not remain idle. He is not satisfied merely to honor the soul with His presence; He sanctifies it with His power and, with the cooperation of

---

91 - John 14:23.

the soul, He works in it all the good that is necessary for its salvation.

In this way, the Holy Spirit governs the soul as the father of a family rules his house; He instructs the soul like a teacher at school; He cultivates the garden of the soul as a gardener works the soil; He reigns in the soul like a ruler in his state; and He illumines the soul as the sun enlightens the world. He is, in a word, like the very soul in the body, which gives life and movement, although not as a substance informing matter. Like a fire, He illumines our intellect and inflames our will. Like a dove, He makes us simple, meek, compliant, and mutual friends. Like a cloud, He protects us against the heat of the flesh and tempers the violence of our passions. Like a soft breeze, He inclines our will to good and removes it from evil. As a result, the just Christian abhors the vices which he previously loved and begins to love the virtues which he once hated, as we see in the case of David, who hated iniquity and loved and delighted in the ways of the Lord.[92]

In this way, grace renders man capable of all good! It smooths the path to heaven and makes God's yoke sweet, thus enabling man to run along the way of the virtues. It also restores and heals his wounded nature and thereby makes that light which in his weakened condition seemed heavy. In an ineffable manner it arms him with the supernatural virtues that illumine the intellect,

92 - Ps. 118:14; 104.

inflame and fortify the will, temper the concupiscible appetite, and rectify the irascible appetite.

Note carefully what the Lord promises to do for us if we turn to Him: "The Lord Your God will circumcise your heart and the heart of your seed, so you may love the Lord your God with all your heart and with all your soul, so that you will live."[93] But how is it that He promises to do this for us, when at another time He commanded that we ourselves must love God with our whole heart and soul? If God will do this for us, why does He command us to do it? And if we must do it, how can He promise to do it for us?

The difficulty is resolved by St. Augustine: "Lord, give me the grace to do what You command me to do and command me to do what You will." God commands us to do what we ought to do and He likewise gives us the grace to do it. Hence, at one and the same time there is a command and a promise. God and man perform the same action together, He as the first cause and man as a secondary cause. In this regard God is like an artist who guides the brush in the hand of a student in order to help him paint a picture. Both produce the work but each contributes to the effect in a different manner. God acts with us, always protecting our liberty, but after the work is finished, man has no reason to boast for himself, rather, he should glorify God in the words of the prophet: "Lord, You will give us peace, for You have fashioned all our works for us."[94]

---

93 – Deut. 30:6.

94 – Isa. 26:12.

CHAPTER 12

JUSTIFICATION THROUGH GRACE

A S GREAT and numerous as the divine benefits and blessings are, what good are they, O Lord, if they do not awaken me from my sleep and call me to repentance? I have been such an unworthy vessel of the grace You gave me at baptism that I have defiled the temple which You sanctified for Yourself. I have raised in it an altar for the idols of my delights, and I have desecrated it with my evil deeds.

There was a time, my Savior, when I was so blind and lost that I lived as if there were no law and, indeed, as if there were no God. I never thought of death, judgment, or the next life. The law that governed me was the law of my passions. I did whatever I pleased and I desired many other things that I could not obtain. In this way many years of my life have passed, years in which I lived in such heavy darkness that I could almost feel it with my hands. How late have I known You, eternal Light! How late have I opened my eyes to gaze upon Your beauty! Yet, during all those years You endured me and waited patiently for me , because You did not desire death to take me unprepared. O the loftiness of Your judgments and the greatness of Your mercy! How many others have been snatched from this life in the very midst of their sins, to suffer eternal torment, while I, who was also a sinner, have been spared by Your mercy.

What would have become of me if You called me to judgment then? What defense could I have given while I was in that sinful state? O merciful and redeeming Lord, how grateful I am to You, that I am not already numbered among the condemned, as I surely would have been if You snatched me from life during sinful years. Blessed be Your patience through which I live and blessed be Your mercy which has endured me for so long.

Even more, You did not merely wait for me while I lived in sin, but You visited me many times as if I were Your friend, to call me back to You with sweet and secret inspirations. You frequently reminded me of the greatness of my sins, the shortness of this life, the eternity of the life to come, the rigor of Your justice, and the clemency of Your mercy. Your presence would suddenly surprise me even in the midst of my sins, so that even though I persisted in the pursuit of worldly pleasures and wished to eat of the onions of Egypt, You made tears come to my eyes even as I ate. I spent all my time offending You, but

You were equally longing to convert me. In all the paths of my life I fled from You, as if it meant nothing to me to lose You, but You sought and pursued me, as if it were of great importance to find me.

In this way You pursued me for many days, but I responded to Your blessings with curses. All these things were so many voices whereby You sweetly called me and sought to draw me to Yourself. But when these voices did not suffice, You uttered a loud cry in the ears of my soul, commanding me to rise from my sin and return from death to life. It was a voice filled with power and mercy, for if it is the greatest mercy to pardon sinners, it is the greatest power to make them just.

No one, Lord, can have certitude in this life that he is justified, for no man knows whether he is worthy of hatred or love. But a man can have a greater or less degree of moral certainty, according to the signs of justification and the manifestations of Your grace. And not the least of these signs is the fact that a man has abandoned his evil ways and has persevered for a long time without being conscious of mortal sin or any attachment to mortal sin. Any Christian who recognizes this or any of the other signs of justification in himself should give You thanks for so singular a blessing! Let them speak to you in this way:

"May You be blessed forever, dearest Lord, and most generous Benefactor. In spite of what I am and have been, You, in Your great mercy has given me the Spirit of Your grace as the sign of adoption and the pledge of eternal life. Through Him my soul receives You as Spouse and is clothed in beauty and strength, so that it may be pleasing in Your sight and terrible to the demons.

"Blessed be the day that such a Guest entered into my house and blessed be the hour in which the doors of my soul were thrown open to receive Him. Truly that was the day of my birth and my own Christmas, for then the Son of God was born in my soul. It was also my Easter, because on that day I rose from death to life. And it was the day of my Pentecost, because then I received the Holy Spirit. Let Job curse the day of his conception and birth because he was born a slave of sin and son of wrath; I shall praise and sing with joy for this second day, and I shall pray that the memory of it will always remain with me, because on that day the Lord freed me from sin.

"This is the day on which the angels sing for the conversion of the sinner, the pious mother rejoices over the talent that has been found, the Good Shepherd rejoices over the finding of the lost sheep, and the devils weep because of the prize that has been snatched from them. This is the day on which the heavenly Father receives the Christian as his son, the Son receives him as a brother, the Holy Spirit accepts him as His dwelling place, and the whole court of heaven welcomes him as a future fellow-citizen.

"But if the angels sing for joy on this day, how can my mouth be silent, my tongue be mute, and my lips not sing with praise? All those canticles, rejoicings, and thanksgivings that the prophets prescribe at the coming of the Messiah should now be offered by the true penitent for the blessing of his conversion, for now the Son of God has truly come to him.

"To what other blessings, Lord, shall I compare this great benefit? Great was the blessing of creation, wherein You drew me from non-being to being, but still greater is the blessing of justification whereby You drew me from the state of sin to the state of grace. In the first instance You produced a human being, a son of man; in the second, a divine being, a son of God. And not only is it a greater thing to justify a man than to create him, but it is even greater than to create the heavens and the earth, because all these things are limited and finite goods, while the grace of justification is a participation in an infinite good.

"Great is the blessing that we expect in glory, but in its own way justification is no less a blessing, for it is no less remarkable to make a just man out of a sinner than to make a just man blessed. Indeed, there is a greater distance between sin

and grace than between grace and glory. Moreover, redemption is also a great blessing, but what
would it profit a man to be redeemed if he were
not also justified? Justification is the key to all
other blessings; without it, not only are all the
others of no profit to us, but they would become
the basis of a greater condemnation.

"But if this blessing of justification is so great
and if, as I piously hope, I am among those who
are justified, I beseech You, Lord, to tell me why.
Why did You confer so great a blessing on me?
What do You see in me, in whom there is nothing but sin? I did not truly know You; I did not
truly love You; I did not serve You or think of
You. I cannot cease to be astonished, for I find
no other reason for my justification than Your
goodness. And when, in addition to this, I recall
the many companions of my sins, of whom I was
the worst, I see that You rejected some of them
and chose me instead. When I consider this, I
am so deeply moved that I don't know how to
praise You nor how to thank You. I could spend
my whole life asking: Lord, what did You see in
me that was better than the others? You called
me and gazed on me with love, but You left others to their sins, although they were much less
evil than I. I know not what to say or do, except
to thank You in the words of the Psalm: 'You
have broken my bonds. I will sacrifice to You the

sacrifice of praise and I will call upon the name of the Lord.'[95]

"You alone, O Lord, created us from nothing and You alone preserved us in being. So also, through Your Spirit, You enabled us to be reborn through grace and preserved the grace that You gave us. As the prophet says: 'Unless the Lord build the house, they labor in vain that build it. Unless the Lord keep the city, he watches in vain that keep it.'[96] You raised us up from sin and You have kept us from falling back into sin. Therefore, if I have risen from my evil ways, You have given me Your hand, and if now I am standing upright, You support me lest I fall.

"All my good resolutions and inspirations have been blessings from You. As often as I have conquered the enemy or my evil inclinations, it has been through Your help. For if it is true that no one can worthily say 'Jesus' without the special favor of the Holy Spirit and that one can no more perform a meritorious act without Your help than a branch can bear fruit when separated from the vine, it is clear that if this poor branch has produced any fruit of good works, it is because of the vine to which it is joined. If at any time I have done any good work, it is through You that I did

---

95 – Ps. 115:16.

96 – Ps. 126:1-2.

it. You have worked all my works in me, and for all of them I give You thanks and acknowledge that I am Your debtor.

"What shall I say of the numerous opportunities You gave me to live well? How many preachers did You send to instruct me, how many good confessors, holy friends, and good companions! How many good examples and pious books to awaken me to a better life! Who can count the dangers and evils into which I could have fallen, but from which You protected me? There is no sin committed by one man that another man could not commit just as easily. Accordingly, the sins of all men could just as easily have been my sins, for I could have committed those sins if in Your infinite mercy You had not saved me from them. How often, O good Jesus, have You bound the hands of my enemy so that he could not tempt me or, if he tempted me, so that he could not overpower me! How often I could say with the prophet: 'The Lord is my helper. I will not fear what man can do unto me. ... Being pushed, I was overturned that I might fall, but the Lord supported me. The Lord is my strength and my praise and He is become my salvation.'[97]

"How often, through mortal sins, have I deserved to lose your protection, as has happened

---

97 - Ps. 117:6-14.

to others? Surely, there are many reasons why men deserve to be abandoned. The proud man deserves to lose Your grace because he uses it only for his own pride and vainglory. The ungrateful man deserves to lose it because he does not give thanks. The slothful man deserves to be deprived of grace because it is only proper to take it away from a man that does not know how to profit from it. And he who does not keep himself from the occasions of sin, deserves to fall into sin.

"But how can I think that I am free of such faults? So many times I have been vain and proud because of Your gifts to me and have thus stolen the glory that belongs to You alone. I have been ungrateful for Your blessings and slothful and lazy in making use of them. I have been so rash and foolish as to place myself in great danger of sin. Consequently, many times in my life I have deserved for You to abandon me!. But so great is Your patience that You have overlooked my failings and have closed Your eyes to my weakness. Until now You endured me with great patience and hast not willed that any help should be denied me, even when I have repaid You with so many offences. The sorrow and remorse of conscience that would be mine if You wert ever to abandon me, I now convert into thanks and words of praise, saying with the prophet: 'Turn, O my soul, to Your rest, for the Lord hath been bountiful to you. For He delivered my soul from death, my eyes from tears, my feet from falling.'"[98]

Glory to God forever!

---

98 - Ps. 1114:7-8.